relationships

DISCOVER DISCIPLESHIP

WORKBOOK 4: DISCOVER RELATIONSHIPS

Jay Morgan

Discover Discipleship Series:
Work Book Four: Discover Relationships
© Jay Morgan 2019

The views expressed in this book are solely those of the author. Some ideas may be similar to others found elsewhere. In this study they are transcribed into the author's words unless specifically noted. Effort was given to identify and cite sources that influenced the ideas presented. As this study was developed from a lifetime of hearing and reading Christian teaching, as well as over 28 years of ministry by the author, it is possible that an idea was learned, and the source was not remembered or noted. If you believe this is the case, please contact the author or publisher and we will work to correct it.

The author's intent is to offer information of a spiritual nature that will educate the reader in the search for spiritual well-being. The author nor publisher shall have neither liability nor responsibility to any person or entity with respect to any loss or damage caused, or alleged to have been caused, directly or indirectly, by the information contained in this book.

Editors: Heidi Wallenborn and Wendy Smith

ISBN 979-8-9856015-3-4
Printed in the United States of America

Published by: APC Ministries
www.apcwv.com

table of contents

getting the most from this study

We are glad that you have chosen to pursue this course of study, and hope that you are looking forward to beginning. Before you dig in, there are three important things to take into account:

SMALL DAILY INVESTMENT

To get the maximum benefit from this course of study, a 10-15 minute investment to complete a lesson each day is recommended.

Small choices that we make each day create the lives we live. Your commitment to spending a few minutes each day to think, journal, study and learn, is a commitment to planting and watering seeds of change.

By doing this, you are creating a harvest of good fruit in your life for yourself and for others to benefit from over time. Even if you do not continue this study, forming the habit of taking time for daily personal growth will benefit you for the rest of your life.

WEEKLY DISCUSSION WITH OTHERS

Each journey that you take in life, whether physical or spiritual, is more enjoyable you we have companions. Someone may see something that you missed, or have an idea that is different than your own. Travel is almost always safer in groups.

Likewise, we encourage you to meet regularly with another person or a group of people to discuss your thoughts. Spend time with someone who is farther down the spiritual road so that you can learn from and lean on them as you progress along your own path. This road is too serious for you to travel upon alone.

MORE THAN A STUDY

This workbook is the fourth in a series of six. You will find that the six core discoveries as put forth in this series will serve you well beyond this study. These core discoveries are to be used as guides for your spiritual journey, and the workbooks will serve as reference guides throughout your lifetime. The content doesn't end with the course.

Also, keep in mind that each of the six workbooks in this series builds upon each other. It is imperative that you study them in order—and completely—to get the most out of this study.

May God bless you as you increase in your knowledge of Him.

Pastor Jay Morgan

For ongoing support and conversations around the topics contained in the *Discover Discipleship Course*, join our online discussion by searching "Discover Discipleship Tribe" on Facebook.

group guidelines

If you are completing this Study in a group setting, the following guidelines will help keep meetings safe, focused and productive:

GROUP LOGISTICS

Appropriate group size. Ideally a group should consist of 4-6 people: a group leader and apprentice leader who have both previously completed the *Discover Discipleship Course,* and 3-4 new participants. If a group is larger, consider discussing key concepts from the lessons together, and then forming smaller break-out groups to discuss the questions.

Meet consistently. During the first meeting the group should agree upon a day/time each week for the meeting. Weekly meetings are ideal. Avoid routinely canceling meetings.

Plan the material. Decide each week how many days/lessons you will want to work on at the next meeting. It is recommended that you cover 3-5 lessons at each weekly group meeting.

Be prepared. Both the leader and participants should fully engage with each week's planned material, and answer all questions *before* the group meeting.

MEETING LOGISTICS

Meeting agenda. Begin each meeting by briefly connecting with everyone. Read the meeting ground rules (on the next page) and pray. Summarize lesson points, one lesson at a time, and allow ample time to discuss the lesson questions. The questions are key to the effectiveness of this study.

Group Prayer. End each group meeting with a time of extended prayer when possible. Worship together a few minutes and then pray for each other's needs. These times of prayer will most likely develop more after *Workbook 3: Discover Growth.*

Meeting length. Weekly meetings should typically last 1 to 1 1/2 hours. Make sure to always start and *end* the meeting on time. People might want to stay longer than originally planned, however, be mindful that members might have other obligations after the scheduled meeting time.

MEETING GROUND RULES

To help keep meetings focused, safe and productive, begin every meeting by reading these ground rules aloud.

1. **I will commit to make group meetings and this study a priority by being prepared and being on time.** The group meeting is not the time to work on answers to questions. I understand the group meeting will be unproductive if I have not read the lessons and answered the questions before the group meeting.

2. **I will maintain confidentiality.** What is said in the group stays in the group unless someone threatens to hurt themselves or others. In that case, appropriate people will be notified to ensure the safety of all parties involved.

3. **I will refrain from gossiping about others during the group meeting.** I will keep my focus on my experiences and not on other people. I will leave others' names anonymous when sharing my negative personal experiences in the group setting.

4. **I will be honest.** The purpose of this study is to give honest answers and work toward the study of God's truth. Everyone is here to discover God's truth together. We cannot discover truth until we ask questions and seek answers.

5. **I will respect the other members of the group.** I will refrain from being on electronic devices, interrupting others and / or having side conversations.

6. **I understand that my role is not to "save" or "fix" anyone else.** Together, our role is to continue to point each other toward Jesus and the truth of His teachings.

Go to the *Church Leader Resources* section of **www.discoverdiscipleship. com** for additional resources to assist with leading a productive group meeting.

introduction to relationships

Jesus replied: "Love the Lord your God with all your heart

and with all your soul and with all your mind."

This is the first and greatest commandment.

And the second is like it: "Love your neighbor as yourself." —MATTHEW 22:36-39

the relationship decision

Congratulations on making it to the fourth discovery of your spiritual journey. We are glad you have chosen to continue this study and hope you are looking forward to discovering more spiritual truths.

REVIEW

In *Workbook 1: Discover Identity*, we learned that we are created in the image of God as His children. God desires to have a family to share eternity with. Because of sin, we have all experienced spiritual death. This spiritual death brings physical death and eternal separation from God. Because we have lost our identity as God's children, we seek security, worth and fulfillment from alternative sources—people, things, or even our own self-perception. This search leads us further into sin and away from God.

Motivated by His love for us, God came to us through Jesus and did everything possible to restore us to Himself. When we surrender our will to Jesus' Lordship, the Holy Spirit comes into us and rebirths the child of God in us. Our sins are forgiven, and we are restored to a relationship with God. Remember, as a spiritually reborn child of God, we have new desires and interests.

As a child of God you will desire the following:

- More of God and less of sin. (Galatians 5:17)

- Intimacy with the Father and the nourishment of the Word of God. (Romans 8:15-16, 1 Peter 2:2)

- The community of God's family. (Ephesians 2:19)

- To bear the image of God in the world and do the works you were created to do. (Ephesians 2:8-10, Matthew 28:18-20)

- To honor God with all of your life and resources.
  (1 Corinthians 6:19-20)

The purpose of the *Discover Discipleship Course* is to help you develop these desires. They were placed in you by God, but you have to cooperate with God and allow these desires to mature and grow. Living in your identity as God's child and allowing these desires to develop will help you discover true security, worth and fulfillment.

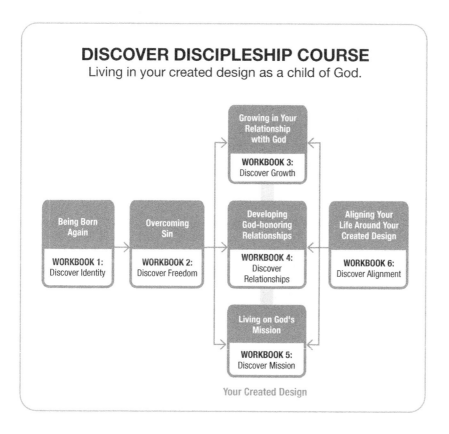

DISCOVER DISCIPLESHIP COURSE
Living in your created design as a child of God.

Growing in Your Relationship wtith God

WORKBOOK 3:
Discover Growth

Being Born Again

WORKBOOK 1:
Discover Identity

Overcoming Sin

WORKBOOK 2:
Discover Freedom

Developing God-honoring Relationships

WORKBOOK 4:
Discover Relationships

Aligning Your Life Around Your Created Design

WORKBOOK 6:
Discover Alignment

Living on God's Mission

WORKBOOK 5:
Discover Mission

Your Created Design

In *Workbook 2: Discover Freedom*, we learned that although we are spiritually reborn as God's children, we still have spiritual strongholds—old, destructive, sinful desires. These strongholds are formed over a lifetime of allowing *substitute identities*, rather than our identity as God's child, define us.

We must cooperate with the Holy Spirit to experience freedom from these strongholds. By taking personal responsibility for change, seeking God's power to change, finding partners to support our change and developing a plan for change, we can experience freedom from spiritual strongholds.

In *Workbook 3: Discover Growth*, we learned how to develop our relationship with God. We understand that God not only initiated a relationship with us through Christ, but He continues to initiate a relationship with us through the Holy Spirit.

As with all relationships, a relationship with God must be cultivated. Our relationship with God grows as we learn to listen to Him and spend time with Him in worship, prayer and Bible study. As the influence of His Spirit grows stronger in our lives, our need to pursue security, worth and fulfillment in *substitute identities* grows smaller as we are defined by being His child.

THE RELATIONSHIP DECISION

Loving God and living in freedom as His child is only part of what God desires for you. Look at the following verse:

> One of them, an expert in the law, tested him with this question: "Teacher, which is the greatest commandment in the Law?" Jesus replied: "Love the Lord your God with all your heart and with all your soul and with all your mind." This is the first and greatest commandment. And the second is like it: "Love your neighbor as yourself."
> — **Matthew 22:35-39**

Notice that Jesus taught that loving God is the first and greatest commandment, but loving people is a close second.

In this workbook, you will learn to make the next Core Decision of your Spiritual Journey.

The Relationship Decision:
I choose to honor God in my human relationships by changing my attitude toward others, giving and receiving forgiveness, handling conflict Jesus' way and by becoming an active part of God's family.

unity lost and restored

When God created Adam and placed him in the Garden of Eden, Adam enjoyed an intimate relationship with God and was given a fulfilling purpose here on earth. But God did not want him to be alone. So, God created Eve. This was the gift of human community.

A simple definition for community is to have a *common unity*. Community is found when parts learn to function as a unit. Adam and Eve existed in this state of oneness with God and with each other.

UNITY LOST

When Adam and Eve sinned and separated themselves from God, the first thing they lost was their unity with God. They felt naked and ashamed in God's Presence.

> He (Adam) answered, "I heard you in the garden, and I was afraid because I was naked; so I hid." — **Genesis 3:10**

The next thing they lost was their unity with each other. When God questioned them about their sin, Adam immediately blamed God and Eve for his mistakes.[1]

> The man said, "The woman you put here with me — she gave me some fruit from the tree, and I ate it. — **Genesis 3:12**

Their loss was not just theirs; it spread to all humanity.

> When Adam sinned, sin entered the world. Adam's sin brought death, so death spread to everyone, for everyone sinned.
> — **Romans 5:12 NLT**

Adam and Eve's first son killed their second son. As we read just a few verses further into Genesis, we see the continued deterioration of human relationships as people begin to lord over each other, exploit each other, and hurt each other. The common unity humanity had with God and with each other is lost.

1. What are your thoughts regarding the concept that sin not only separates people from God, it also separates us from each other?

UNITY RESTORED

According to Scripture, Jesus came to restore unity. He came to restore our relationship with God, and He also came to destroy divisions between people.

> "My prayer is not for them alone. I pray also for those who will believe in me through their message, that all of them may be one, Father, just as you are in me and I am in you. May they also be in us so that the world may believe that you have sent me. I have given them the glory that you gave me, *that they may be one as we are one —I in them and you in me — so that they may be brought to complete unity.* Then the world will know that you sent me and have loved them even as you have loved me.
> — **John 17:20-23** *(Emphasis added)*

> There is neither Jew nor Gentile, neither slave nor free, nor is there male and female, for you are all one in Christ Jesus. — **Galatians 3:28**

> For He (Jesus) himself is our peace, who has
> made the two groups one and has destroyed
> the barrier, the dividing wall of hostility.
> —Ephesians 2:14

Through Jesus, every spiritually reborn child of God becomes part
of God's family and is restored to community with God and with
each other.[2]

> For through him we both have access to the
> Father by one Spirit. Consequently, you are
> no longer foreigners and strangers, but fellow
> citizens with God's people and also members of
> his household. — Ephesians 2:18-19

2. **Was the concept that Jesus came to repair your human
   relationships, and not just your relationship with God,
   emphasized or de-emphasized in your past church
   experience? Explain:**

how to love others

Let's re-read Jesus' explanation of what God wants from us:

> One of them, an expert in the law, tested him with this question: "Teacher, which is the greatest commandment in the Law?" Jesus replied: "Love the Lord your God with all your heart and with all your soul and with all your mind." This is the first and greatest commandment. And the second is like it: "Love your neighbor as yourself."
> — Matthew 22: 35-39

Notice the second greatest commandment: "Love your neighbor as yourself." Loving others like yourself seems impossible. After all, others aren't as "lovable" as you, right? So, how is it possible to love people the way Christ instructed?

Develop a passionate relationship with God. The first step in loving others as yourself is to realize that your love for people must flow from God's love in you. God loves you with an unfailing love. Through the cross He proved there is nothing you can ever do to make Him love you more than He already does.

You must allow His love to shape the way you see the world, people and yourself. Only when you fully experience His kind of love can you fully love others. Only when you accept your value can you truly value others. This requires a vibrant relationship with God.

As you understand God's great love for you and accept your value, the way you see others is transformed. When your love for others flows from love given by God, you will stop expecting people to fulfill needs that only God can.

1. What does it mean for your love for people to flow from God's love?

View others as loved by God. When you have experienced God's love and are reborn as His child, you should no longer try to use a relationship with another person as your source of security, worth and fulfillment. Your security, worth and fulfillment now come from God's love, and by living in your created design as His child. Relationships with people should no longer define you. You are defined by your identity as a child of God, made in His image.

Although people no longer define who we are, we do need each other.

> The Lord God said, "It is not good for the man to be alone. I will make a helper suitable for him." — **Genesis 2:18**

2. According to the previous verse, humans exist to _____ each other.

> So God created mankind in his own image, in the image of God he created *them*; male and female he created them. God blessed *them* and said to *them*, "Be fruitful and increase in number; fill the earth and subdue it. Rule over the fish in the sea and the birds in the sky and over every living creature that moves on the ground." — **Genesis 1:27-28** *(Emphasis added)*

Notice that the mission of subduing and ruling over the earth was given to Adam and Eve, not just Adam. They were to be helpers—companions—to each other as they fulfilled their God-given purpose on earth.

This means that other people do not solely exist for your benefit. Each person is made by God and loved by God and made for His purpose and glory. Each of us is made in God's image. Each of us is uniquely designed to fulfill God's purpose. This also means that God loves others as much as He loves you. Even people who dishonor God with their lives and are separated from Him because of their sin were made by God. He desires to see them home as well. (II Peter 3:9)

When you recognize others' value and know how much God loves them, you can let go of your agenda for them and learn to truly love them the way you love yourself. You learn to become a companion—a helper, a servant—to them as they fulfill God's will as well.

3. How does knowing that other people were made for God's purposes and do not exist solely for your benefit, change your view and expectations of them?

View yourself as a companion (or helper) to others. In order to treat people in a way that honors God and build "common unity" with them, you must see yourself as their companion. The word companion begins with the prefix "com" which means *with*. [3] In other words, life should be shared with people. We are God's children made in God's image, helping each other fulfill our God-given purpose on earth.

4. What does it mean to be a helper, or companion, to others as you fulfill your God-given purposes together?

To help others means you learn to serve them and meet their needs. Notice how the following passage describes Christ's servant attitude and challenges us to be the same way with each other:

> Do nothing out of selfish ambition or vain conceit. Rather, in humility value others above yourselves, not looking to your own interests but each of you to the interests of the others. In your relationships with one another, have the same mindset as Christ Jesus: Who, being in very nature God, did not consider equality with God something to be used to his own advantage; rather, he made himself nothing by taking the very nature of a servant, being made in human likeness. And being found in appearance as a man, he humbled himself by becoming obedient to death—even death on a cross! — **Philippians 2:3-8**

5. How would you treat people differently if you applied the preceding passage to your relationships?

Next, we will examine eight *Relational Attitudes*—and the beliefs that motivate them—that inhibit us from becoming a companion to others.

notes

relational attitudes

In your relationships with one another, have the same mindset as Christ Jesus: ...he made himself nothing by taking the very nature of a servant... — PHILIPPIANS 2:5, 7a

the confined attitude

Confined means *restricted, limited.*[4] People with a confined attitude toward relationships live restricted from others and depend mainly upon themselves. They might have relationships, but usually refuse to connect deeply.

We will take longer studying the confined attitude than we will the other attitudes because it can help us understand our need to both give and receive companionship.

CHALLENGING THE CONFINED ATTITUDE WITH THE TRUTH

You are not alone in the world. If you have a confined attitude toward relationships you probably feel alone, which is a natural outcome of isolating yourself from others. Choosing to isolate yourself from others is often motivated by the fear of being rejected or hurt. Suffering, pain or disappointment in relationships makes keeping everyone at a distance seem safer than risking getting hurt.

To move beyond the feeling of being alone, first grasp the reality that God has always been with you. He has led you, helped you, picked you up. Even when you could not feel His presence, He was there.

> It was I who taught Ephraim to walk, taking them by the arms; but they did not realize it was I who healed them. I led them with cords of human kindness, with ties of love. To them I was like one who lifts a little child to the cheek, and I bent down to feed them. — **Hosea 11:3-4**

You may have felt deserted by God because He did not stop others from hurting you. But He was with you each moment.

> You keep track of all my sorrows. You have collected all my tears in your bottle. You have recorded each one in your book.
> — **Psalm 56:8 NLT**

We may never understand why God does not stop people from abusing their free will to harm others; but we do know He promises healing, and He promises that one day He will settle the score.

> "But I will restore you to health and heal your wounds," declares the Lord. — **Jeremiah 30:17a**

> Do not take revenge, my dear friends, but leave room for God's wrath, for it is written: "It is mine to avenge; I will repay," says the Lord.
> —**Romans 12:19**

1. **Has being hurt, or the fear of being hurt, caused you to withdraw from relationships? If yes, explain:**

Whether or not you realize it, others have helped you get where you are in life. It may seem that you always had to care for yourself. You may feel that people always let you down. But not everyone has let you down all the time.

Think about it. Someone fed and carried you and changed your diapers. Someone taught you in school or taught you a skill. Someone took a chance on you to hire you or buy your products. You did not fall from the sky, hatch yourself under a rock, and raise yourself in the wild. You did not get where you are in life entirely by yourself.

Overcoming this belief begins with looking around and returning help to people who have *already* helped you. When you think you have done it all on your own (and you may have done a lot), you end up neglecting people who have invested in you.

> ...Freely you have received; freely give.
> — Matthew 10:8b

2. **List a few people who have invested in you over the course of your life. Next to each name list something you can do to be a companion (helper) to them.**

You are called by God to be a companion to others. You might think that being a companion—a helper—to others is only meant for extroverted, social people. The Scriptural call for companionship is not just given to extroverts. Whether you are an extrovert who is energized by social interaction or an introvert who needs to recharge between social interactions, remember that God gave you gifts to use in service to others along with a unique way of interacting with people.

Scripture insists that people need you and that you need people.

Two are better than one, because they have a
good return for their labor: if either of them
falls down, one can help the other up. But pity
anyone who falls and has no one to help them
up. Also, if two lie down together, they will
keep warm. But how can one keep warm alone?
Though one may be overpowered, two can
defend themselves. A cord of three strands is
not quickly broken. — **Ecclesiastes 4:9-12**

Carry each other's burdens, and in this way
you will fulfill the law of Christ.
— **Galatians 6:2**

Remember, like a lion stalking prey, Satan waits for you to become
isolated and alone, and then jumps in for the kill. Do not be ignorant of his tricks. Build strong relationships with safe people.

Be alert and of sober mind. Your enemy the
devil prowls around like a roaring lion looking
for someone to devour. — **I Peter 5:8**

3. **Is it easy or hard for you to build relationships? Why?**

4. **In what ways has approaching life on your own left you
   weak and/or vulnerable?**

Building relationships with others and receiving help from them does not mean you are weak or lazy. When you build relationships, you are NOT asking others to do for you what you should do for yourself. You are NOT creating complete dependency on others.

Here is a simple illustration of how healthy relationships work:

- Imagine a solitary board standing upright by itself. How stable is it standing by itself? It does not take much pressure to knock it over. This is the confined attitude.

- Now imagine two boards leaning against each other at the top, like an upside-down V. They are dependent upon each other. If one falls, the other falls with it. This is the codependent attitude we will learn about next.

- Lastly, imagine a framed wall. Several boards standing strong, connected to other boards and anchored to the floor. If one board falls it may weaken the wall, but the other boards will not necessarily fall with it. This is companionship: linking your strengths to others' strengths.

Companionship means you are able to give into the lives of others and receive from others. No one can do everything well. When you are too proud to accept what others have to offer, you are not as strong and effective as you could be.

> As iron sharpens iron, so one person sharpens another. — **Proverbs 27:17**

In strong companionships, where one is weak the other is strong, and vice versa. Linked together, we are stronger than we are apart. Each part of our physical body does something that the other parts are not designed to do. When all parts work together based upon their strengths, the entire body benefits. This is also how it works in the Body of Christ—the Church.

> The eye cannot say to the hand, "I don't need you!" And the head cannot say to the feet, "I don't need you!" — **1 Corinthians 12:21**

5. Is it easier for you to give help or receive help? Why?

6. How can the Confined Attitude limit or keep you from
    serving others the way Jesus did?

the codependent attitude

Codependent means *having an excessive emotional or psychological reliance upon a partner.*[5] It is having one's sense of well-being tied to someone else's attention, approval and/or affection. Although this attitude is different from the Confined Attitude, it is not uncommon for someone who is normally confined in their relationships to form an unhealthy codependent reliance.

The Codependent Attitude brings together two extremes: *the Damsel (or the Dude) in Distress* and *the Rescuer.* The first is always in crisis and the second finds validation by rescuing the one in crisis.[6]

CHALLENGING THE CODEPENDENT ATTITUDE WITH THE TRUTH

You can be alone. If you fear being alone, you may stay in a harmful relationship and put up with more pain than you ever should. You may even allow yourself to be abused.

Overcoming the fear of being alone starts with a solid relationship with God. Understand that God is the true Source of your security and worth. As you learn to trust Him in this truth, your expectations of human relationships change. No one can give you what only God can. Remember, human relationships should flow *from* your relationship with God. He will bring the right people into your life as you trust and obey Him.

1. How will developing a strong relationship with God help you overcome the fear of being alone?

You can learn to do things for yourself. As we learned in the previous lesson, we do need others and we can benefit from their strengths. But be aware that you might expect others to do for you what you should do for yourself. If you are not joining your strengths with their strengths, you are leaning too heavily on them. (Remember the upside down "V"?) Also, be aware that when you take the role of the *Rescuer Codependent,* you might do for others what they should do for themselves.

> Carry each other's burdens, and in this way you will fulfill the law of Christ. If anyone thinks they are something when they are not, they deceive themselves. Each one should test their own actions. Then they can take pride in themselves alone, without comparing themselves to someone else, *for each one should carry their own load.*
> — **Galatians 6:2-5** *(Emphasis added)*

There are times when circumstances, injuries or illness might incapacitate us or limit what we can do. In these times we have no choice but to rely on others more than what is normally expected. But even in these times, we should learn to do what we can do, play to our strengths and refuse to stop trying. And remember, not all strengths are physical.

The following four steps will help you overcome the fear of doing things for yourself.

- Learn to trust God.

- Learn all you can from others.

- Do everything you can do for yourself.

- Ask people for help when this is not enough.

2. Have you expected others to carry your load without attempting to carry it yourself? If yes, in what ways?

You are not useless if you are not "fixing" someone. If you take the *Rescuer's Codependent* attitude, you often try to rescue someone because your sense of worth comes from trying to "fix" other people.

To accept that you have a useful purpose that does not involve enabling others to be weak, remember that your worth and fulfillment come from a relationship with God. When you base your worth on other people's opinions or seek fulfillment in what you can accomplish in others, you will be left empty. Someone else will expect from you what only God can give.

Never attempt to do for people what only God can do for them. Ultimately, people's answers are found in a relationship with God. When you try to be their rescuer you are trying to fulfill a need in them that only God can. This is too big a need for any person to fill. You can, however, be a companion by pointing them to the truth and encourage their growth. Show them how to stand on their own two feet. Do not do for others what they are capable of doing for themselves. (Review the previous section.)

3. Identify ways that you have felt validated by rescuing or fixing others.

It's okay if someone is unhappy with you. A codependent mindset makes you feel that you need to make sure everyone likes or approves of you. This can lead to taking on the role of a relational *martyr*, consistently putting others' needs before your own while hurting yourself.

To be clear, this does not mean that you should start being rude or insensitive and never care for others. That is the opposite extreme and it is also not like Christ. Scripture tells us to speak truth in love—that is truth motivated by love.

> Instead, speaking the truth in love, we will grow to become in every respect the mature body of him who is the head, that is, Christ.
> — **Ephesians 4:15**

The following verse teaches that if you really love someone, you will speak the truth to them, even if it is painful. But do so with love.

> Wounds from a sincere friend are better than many kisses from an enemy.
> — **Proverbs 27:6 NLT**

What this means is that when you are defined by what Christ said about you through the cross–by your identity as a child of God–the need for human approval becomes less important. You are willing to allow people to be unhappy with you if the truth you are speaking is healthier for them. This is true love.

When we enable destructive behaviors in others, we often think it is motivated by love for them, when actually it is often motivated by our own fears. We are afraid of being rejected, or we are afraid of what it will mean to us if we speak the truth. So, rather than confront people with the truth of their actions and the consequences, we overlook issues or make excuses for them.

4. Which destructive behaviors have you enabled in others because you were afraid of rejection or were afraid of what it would mean for you if you confronted them?

5. How will developing a stronger relationship with God help you overcome the need for human validation?

6   In what ways can a Codependent Attitude limit or keep you from serving others the way that Jesus did?

the controlling attitude

To control means *to restrain or restrict, to dominate, to command.*[7] With a Controlling Attitude you try to force people to do what you believe is right, or what will benefit you. This can come through outright aggression and/or intimidation and/or through subtle manipulation.

CHALLENGING THE CONTROLLING ATTITUDE WITH THE TRUTH

You are not solely responsible for the outcome of someone else's life. You may find that you try to control other people's lives because you believe that you are more responsible for them than you actually are. This can, but does not always, flow from being a *Rescuer* in a codependent relationship. Scripture teaches that in the end, you are only responsible for your own actions.

> So then, each of us will give an account of ourselves to God. — **Romans 14:12**

> God "will repay each person according to what they have done. — **Romans 2:6**

You are not responsible to run or finish anyone's race but your own. You are only responsible to be a companion—a helper—to others while they run their races. Be careful to not become so fixated on how someone else is failing to run *their* own race that you fail to complete *your* race. This does not mean that you ignore others and adopt an "every man for himself" mentality. It does mean that you cannot *force* someone to accept your help and guidance.

As a companion to others, you have a responsibility to offer help, warn, assist and gently restore them to the right path when they stumble. But you cannot make them run in the right direction. You may need to have an honest conversation with someone and explain your concerns, but they must decide for themselves. In other words, *you are not responsible for the outcome of their life.* They must take responsibility for their own race.

Remember that attempting to control others is attempting to play God. When you think you control people, you are usually only fooling yourself anyway. No matter how hard you try to manage someone else's behaviors and make them do what you believe is right, they will usually find a way to do what they want. You cannot change people, but you can change how you view and treat them.

1. How have you tried and failed to force someone else to make a right decision?

You do not always have to clean up other people's messes. Many times, we try to control people's actions because we get frustrated by cleaning up the messes created by their actions. Again, this is rooted in feeling more responsible for someone than you actually are. You have to be willing to let them make their own decisions *and bear the consequences,* no matter how painful. This means that they are free to choose but they are also free to bear the consequences of their choices.

Sometimes people have not had the opportunity to learn from the consequences of their choices because you have shielded them from bearing those penalties. When you shield people from consequences you enable them to keep making destructive decisions.

In other words, sometimes God is trying to shape someone's character by allowing them to feel the magnitudes of their actions, but they never learn the lesson because you are in the way. Get out of the way.[8]

So, as a companion you can warn, suggest and offer help, but you cannot force others to do the right thing. But this also means that you do not have to be harmed or bear the consequences of their choices. In other words, you cannot control others, but you can control what you allow them to do to you.

SIDE NOTE FOR PARENTS: You are responsible for your children while they are young, but part of this responsibility is helping them learn to take responsibility for their behaviors and learn consequences for them. It is critical that children learn healthy boundaries and consequences for their actions while they are young and still in a safe environment. This is done by clearly explaining rules and the appropriate consequences for keeping and breaking those rules, then enforcing the appropriate consequences. Obviously, children do not like to be told, "No," but when they learn healthy boundaries at a young age, it is easier than having to learn them later in life. It also keeps them safer from the possibility of suffering life-altering or fatal consequences as adults.

2. Think of someone in your life whom you have been trying to force to do the "right thing." Why do you feel responsible for the outcome of their life?

3. In what ways can you be a companion to them without enabling them or bearing their consequences for them?

4. In what ways can the Controlling Attitude limit or keep you from serving others the way Jesus did?

the critical attitude

Critical means *inclined to express adverse or disapproving comments or judgements.*[9] It is an attitude marked by disapproval and finding faults. The Critical Attitude focuses on other people's shortcomings. If you take a Critical Attitude you will likely become extremely negative and focus on what is wrong around you.

CHALLENGING THE CRITICAL ATTITUDE WITH THE TRUTH

Your way is not always the only way. If you view life from a critical perspective, you are generally annoyed by other people's actions, mannerisms and / or behaviors and often feel the need to correct others.

> For by the grace given me I say to every one of you: Do not think of yourself more highly than you ought, but rather think of yourself with sober judgment, in accordance with the faith God has distributed to each of you.
> — **Romans 12:3**

Maybe it is true that a lot and people around you often make foolish decisions; it could also be true that you incorrectly assume your way is always the best way. At the root of this judgmental criticism is arrogance. *Different does not necessarily mean deficient.*

1. Do you find it easy to point out what is wrong around you? Explain:

Pointing out other people's faults does not make you less guilty of your own. Pointing out other people's flaws can make you feel better about your own shortcomings. You may think things such as, *"I may have messed up, but at least I'm not as bad as that person."* It is important to remember that your identity is being a child of God through Christ. He is the Source of your worth, not a feeling of superiority over others. Pointing out someone else's sin does not make you less guilty of your own sin.

> As it is written: "There is no one righteous, not even one; — **Romans 3:10**

Scripture is clear that you should consider your own shortcomings as the biggest and work on them before thinking you are in a position to comment on your neighbor's. When you admit and confront your own faults, you are better equipped to help someone else overcome theirs.

> Why do you look at the speck of sawdust in your brother's eye and pay no attention to the plank in your own eye? How can you say to your brother, "Brother, let me take the speck out of your eye," when you yourself fail to see the plank in your own eye? You hypocrite first take the plank out of your eye, and then you will see clearly to remove the speck from your brother's eye. — **Luke 6:41-42**

Paul kept his ego in check by referring to himself as the worst of sinners whom God still saved.

> Here is a trustworthy saying that deserves full
> acceptance: Christ Jesus came into the world to
> save sinners—of whom I am the worst.
> — 1 Timothy 1:15

The closer we get to Christ, the more aware we become of our shortcomings and the more thankful we are that He loves us and is changing us. As we become more accurately self-aware, we become less critical of others.

2. In what ways does being more aware of your own sins and shortcomings change the way you treat others?

CRITICISM VS. RESTORATION

There *are* appropriate times for a believer to point out the faults of another believer and challenge them to change. It is important to remember that while we are to preach the truth about sin and warn every one of its consequences, we cannot hold an unbeliever accountable to live as a Christian. The world cannot be expected to honor the truth because they have not surrendered to Jesus and do not have His Spirit living in them, changing them. However, we are called to hold other *believers* accountable to God's Word.

> It isn't my responsibility to judge outsiders, but
> it certainly is your responsibility to judge those
> inside the church who are sinning. God will
> judge those on the outside; but as the Scriptures
> say, "You must remove the evil person from
> among you." — I Corinthians 5:12-13 NLT

Understand the truth about being judgmental. Many believers incorrectly assume that it is wrong for Christians to tell other Christians they are doing something wrong because that is "judging" them. The previous passage clearly states that the Church has a right to judge those who are part of the Church. To judge means: *to pronounce an opinion concerning right and wrong.*[10] The Church must teach what is right or wrong according to the truth of the Word of God.

> "Do not judge according to appearance, but judge with righteous judgment." — **John 7:24**

It is true that Jesus taught against elevating yourself by condemning others (Matthew 7:1-4). But in the rest of this passage, He also taught that we can tell if a person is truly His by their actions (Matthew 7:15-23). He said many confess Him as Lord with their mouths, but He has never known them. He even warned us to be careful of deceivers and "wolves in sheep's clothing." He taught that we can tell the real from the fake by their actions. In other words, Jesus was not stating that we are never allowed to say that an action is sinful.

Also, notice this verse:

> Brothers and sisters, if someone is caught in a sin, you who live by the Spirit should restore that person gently. But watch yourselves, or you also may be tempted. — **Galatians 6:1**

How can you restore your fellow Christian back to the right path if you are not allowed to tell them that they sinned in the first place?

Read John 8:1-11 in your Bible.

Jesus told the woman that He did not condemn her; but He also instructed her to leave her life of sin. Was He being wrongfully judgmental by pointing out that she was *living a life of sin?*

3. In what ways does this differ from what you thought about passing judgement on others?

Examine your attitude and motive. The Scripture passages from today's lesson teach us that the attitude and motives motivating the confrontation of sin are very important. The goal of criticism and condemnation is typically to either push the person down by pointing out their flaws, or it is to elevate yourself by showing that you are superior in knowledge or actions. Critically pointing out flaws is rooted in pride. Jesus repeatedly taught against prideful condemnation (Reference Luke 18:9-14 and Matthew 7:1-4.)

The condemner can often be unaware that their motives are fueled by pride. This is why you should carefully examine your motives and attitude before criticizing or confronting others.

First, evaluate if the person should be confronted over their actions. Is the matter in question just your preference or is it actually a character or sin issue that should be confronted? What is your reason for confronting them? Is it to help them back onto the right path or is to show what you know?

When you confront sin as a companion in life, you are gently reaching over to help your fallen friend get back up; the motivation is assistance—not arrogance. Companions want to help others grow, not humiliate them for their sin.

If they refuse to get back up and/or acknowledge their sin, there are other steps to take. We will learn more about this on *Day 19: Biblical Conflict Resolution.* But all of this should still be done in the spirit of love seeking restoration, not in a spirit of pride seeking punishment.

4. Reread Galatians 6:1 above. What does this passage teach concerning our attitude when confronting sin?

5. What is the difference between criticizing and restoring?

6. List some ways that the Critical Attitude can limit or keep you from serving others the way Jesus did.

the crisis attitude

A crisis is an *emotionally significant event or radical change of status in a person's life.*[11] Viewing life from a crisis perspective makes even small disappointments seem crisis–significant or radically life-changing. If you have a Crisis Attitude you will frequently find yourself feeling victimized by life and people, and you will have difficulty maintaining long-term relationships.

CHALLENGING THE CRISIS ATTITUDE WITH THE TRUTH

Everyone is not out to get you. When you have suffered a hurt or trauma, or if you were raised in a family that experienced trauma, it is easy to be suspicious of others and believe that they intend to take advantage of or hurt you. This makes maintaining long-term relationships difficult. It may be true that some people have caused you pain and difficulty; but if you believe that everyone is your enemy, you must learn to look at others and yourself differently.

If you take a Crisis Attitude, you may unconsciously cause the crises you have with others. If you believe that people are out to get you, you are likely to act defensively. Others will avoid you, so your idea of being disliked is reinforced.

Then, when you do enter into a relationship, you often put unrealistic expectations on the other person, thinking that perhaps they will be the "perfect" friend or companion you have been searching for. Inevitably, they will let you down. You will feel betrayed which will reaffirm your belief that people are out to harm you. The truth is that if you always look for a reason to leave a relationship you will find one. If you always look for a reason to be suspicious, you will find one.

Another factor that causes constant crisis is becoming emotionally attached to people too quickly—*before* you know if they are reliable.

RULE OF THUMB: Do not become emotionally attached to someone you cannot trust. Do not trust someone you cannot rely on. Do not rely on someone you do not know.[12]

Give people small opportunities to show that they are reliable. Do not expect them to be perfect but consider how they treat you. Do they make sincere efforts to follow through on what they say? If they follow through, begin trusting them with small things and let them demonstrate their trustworthiness.

This does not mean that you should try to trust and connect with everyone. However, in order to be a companion to others you must learn to give people the opportunity to prove their trustworthiness. If you believe that others are *always* trying to hurt you, you will never give them the opportunity to prove themselves. Learn to earnestly pray and ask God to show you if you should trust someone.

> Trust in the Lord with all your heart and lean not on your own understanding; in all your ways submit to him, and he will make your paths straight. — **Proverbs 3:5-6**

1. **Do you tend to do any of the above things that contribute to crises in relationships? If so, underline the parts that apply.**

You are responsible for your own feelings and choices. You are not a victim. If you have a Crisis Attitude in relationships, assigning blame is likely a big issue. You may fall into the trap of believing blame must always be assigned, but rarely assign blame to yourself. You may tend to set yourself up as the "victim" in disagreements and try to make others feel guilty if they stand up for themselves.

You may find it easy to blame others for your feelings and failures and are quick to point out what someone else is doing if you are questioned about your own actions.

You may lie about your actions to avoid blame and operate from an "attack others and defend myself" mindset. You *accuse* others and *excuse* yourself.[13]

In any broken relationship or disagreement, you should consider how much of it was *your* fault, and then *own your part.* You cannot own someone else's part of a problem, but you should own yours.

RULE OF THUMB: *If it is 5 percent your fault, own your 5 percent!* Do not excuse your part – own it, correct it and move forward, even if the other person does not.

2. How quick are you to accept responsibility and correct your mistakes? Give an example.

You are not stuck in life. You can change your situation. The Crisis Attitude can make you feel helpless and victimized. You may complain about your "lot in life" and feel powerless to change it. You will retell stories of betrayal to anyone who will listen. The stories sometimes have merit, but are often small, trivial matters blown out of proportion.

When offered suggestions about how to resolve the problem, you give reasons why those suggestions will not work. You find a *problem* for every *solution*. When offered a solution, you may even get angry because a solution will remove your source of attention and pity. This flows from an unhealthy attachment to attention.

To move away from the Crisis Attitude, first take responsibility for your own actions and life. You have the power to enact change in your life. That power comes through the Holy Spirit and the strength and support of God's family. Review the verses from *Day 4: The Confined Attitude.*

> For it is God who works in you to will and to act in order to fulfill his good purpose.
> — Philippians 2:13

3. In what ways have you felt helpless or victimized?

4. What can you do to feel empowered enough to change your circumstances?

5. How can the Crisis Attitude limit or keep you from serving others in the ways Jesus did?

the competitive attitude

Competitive means *having or displaying a strong desire to be better than others.*[14] A Competitive Attitude is marked by measuring your worth by comparing yourself to others.

CHALLENGING THE COMPETITIVE ATTITUDE WITH THE TRUTH

Worth is not found in being better than others. We are often driven by a need to succeed in one of the *substitute identities* we have studied. *(See Appendix 1: Substitute Identities.)* If you have a Competitive Attitude in relationships, you tend to compare yourself to others and feel validated when you believe you are doing better than they are in one or more of these areas.

1. Review the *Substitute Identity List.* In what ways have you sought validation by being better than someone else in any of these?

To overcome the false belief that worth is found by being better than others, you must first remember the Source of your value and worth as a child of God. True value and worth come from having Christ. *You are no longer defined by human opinion.*

The Bible teaches that each of us has a race to run (Hebrews 12:1). You can waste your time comparing your race to everyone else's, or you can set about running the best race you can. Success is being faithful to complete the task that God has given *you.*

Life is not a competition with others. You must not compare your journey with anyone else's. Your struggle is to do your best, not to be "better" than others. Other people are not your enemies. However, you do have enemies—evil forces that would keep you from fulfilling your mission and completing *your* race.

Remember that you are called to be a companion to others. As long as you view people as competition, you will not be motivated to help them. You perceive their success as your failure. You believe that in order to "win," you need to beat them in life. This can lead to a desire to mess up their race or push them down.

The need to be "better than" others can be subtle, and we can often "spiritualize" it. The attitude can be as simple as feeling validated because your church, beliefs, or morals are "better" than someone else's. Remember that living a life that honors God should influence your actions—not human opinion. Being right in His eyes, not being right and proving others wrong, should be what validates you.

Having someone else's opportunities will not make you more fulfilled. Being jealous of what others have often fuels competitiveness. Remember that God made you unique for a purpose; He fashioned and formed you for a specific job.

> I praise you because I am fearfully and
> wonderfully made; your works are wonderful, I
> know that full well. — **Psalm 139:14**

Someone else's success is *not* your failure. Envying another person's journey, talents or opportunities, however, will guarantee your failure.

> For where you have envy and selfish ambition,
> there you find disorder and every evil practice.
> — **James 3:16**

Failure will come because you became fixated on what you do not have instead of cultivating what you do have. This can be particularly difficult when you feel that life has been unfair while you watch other people squander their opportunities, health, skills, relationships or children that you would love to have. This causes bitterness.

Remember that each of us will answer for our own race. Others will answer for how they cared for or wasted their opportunities, as you will answer for how you cared for or wasted yours.

> When someone has been given much, much will be required in return; and when someone has been entrusted with much, even more will be required. — **Luke 12:48b NLT**

2. **In what ways have other people's opportunities made you feel jealous or angry?**

Faithfulness in *your* journey will determine *your* success. You need to learn to be the person God made you to be and then be a companion to others as they learn to be who they were created to be.

Read Matthew 25:14-30.

3. **How could comparing his assignment to others have contributed to the third servant's failure to complete his assignment?**

4. In what ways has comparing yourself to others kept you from "running your race"?

5. In what ways can a Competitive Attitude limit or keep you from serving others the way that Jesus did?

the consumeristic attitude

To consume means *to use up or expend.*[15] If you take the Consumeristic Attitude toward relationships, you primarily judge and evaluate people and relationships based on what benefit they can provide you.

CHALLENGING THE CONSUMERISTIC ATTITUDE WITH THE TRUTH

People do not exist for your benefit. When you fail to see that we are all fearfully and wonderfully made in God's image for *God's* purposes, it becomes easy to view people as existing for your own purposes. You may then consciously or unconsciously take advantage of them, use them to validate your worth, or exploit them to indulge your appetites.

Obviously, we need things and services other people provide, but you must be aware that you are a companion on *their* journey as well. If you do not recognize this, you will see them as existing to meet your needs.

Notice how Scripture teaches us to view people:

> And the second is like it: "Love your neighbor as yourself." — **Matthew 22:39**

> Do to others as you would have them do to you.
> — **Luke 6:31**

1. **Have you ever been treated as if your only purpose was to provide a service for someone or to please them in some other way? If yes, explain how it made you feel to be used in that way.**

Your relationships do not exist solely for your benefit. It is far too easy to let a consumeristic mindset invade all your relationships rather than seeing the people with whom you are in relationship as companions on your journey:

- People can be considered sexual objects.

- A spouse can be seen as a paycheck or security.

- Friends, family and children can be viewed as trophies to validate worth.

- Employers, employees, clients and customers can be reduced to a means for profit.

Notice the following Scripture instructs us to value others, even above ourselves, just as Jesus does.

> Do nothing out of selfish ambition or vain conceit. Rather, in humility value others above yourselves, not looking to your own interests but each of you to the interests of the others. In your relationships with one another, have the same mindset as Christ Jesus: Who, being in very nature God, did not consider equality with God something to be used to his own advantage; rather, he made himself nothing by taking the very nature of a servant, being made in human likeness. — **Philippians 2:3-7**

Companionship involves both giving and receiving, not simply receiving. It involves serving and meeting the needs of others, not just using them to provide for your own means.

It is not wrong to receive help from others in relationships, but you should also seek opportunities to serve them without expecting them to repay you. This is important with everyone in your life. It is not limited to your friends and close relationships; it includes the cashier, mechanic, bank teller, waitress or anyone else who provides services. Seek ways to serve others rather than only being served.

2. **List people you often overlook or take for granted. Then list at least one way you can serve them this week. Don't forget service personnel, etc.**

LOVING WHEN IT DOESN'T BENEFIT YOU

You are to love others, even if it does not benefit you. Jesus taught that we must treat everyone the same—*with love*—regardless of how they treat us or how we perceive their value to us.

You are to treat people based on your character (that is, the character of Christ in you) rather than *their* behavior.

> But I tell you, love your enemies and pray for those who persecute you, that you may be children of your Father in heaven. He causes his sun to rise on the evil and the good, and sends rain on the righteous and the unrighteous.
> — Matthew 5:44-45

You respond the way you want to be treated; not the way you are treated.

> Do to others as you would have them do to you. — Luke 6:31

You are called to love those who are "unlovable" even if they do not love you in return.

> If you love those who love you, what credit is that to you? Even sinners love those who love them. — **Luke 6:32**

You are called to look out for people who cannot provide any benefit for you in return.

> The King will reply, "Truly I tell you, whatever you did for one of the least of these brothers and sisters of mine, you did for me."
> — **Matthew 25:40**

These actions will help break the habits of a Consumeristic Attitude toward the relationships in your life.

As you learn to accept that *your* needs and wants are not most important; to appreciate the inherent value of all people; and to rely on God as the true Source of your security, fulfillment and worth, you will not feel the need to use others.

3. Review the four preceding passages of Scripture. Based on these, which attitudes or actions do you need to change?

4. How can the Consumeristic Attitude limit or keep you from serving others the way that Jesus did?

the comfortable attitude

Comfortable means *providing physical ease and relaxation.*[16] People who take a Comfortable Attitude look for relationships that place the least stress or strain on them.

CONFRONTING THE COMFORTABLE ATTITUDE WITH THE TRUTH

Different does not always mean deficient. On *Day 7: The Critical Attitude,* we faced the fact that our way is not always the best way. While it is true that we should all conform to the character of Jesus, He has made each of us unique and has shaped us in different ways with different personalities and abilities. Learn to appreciate others' uniqueness instead of criticizing them.

The world teaches you to evaluate people's worth by how they compare to you. You learn to establish pecking orders: [17]

- You consider some people on your level, and you feel comfortable with and around them.

- There are others you believe are more significant than you, so you either tend to avoid them or attempt to impress them.

- Then there are people you believe are inferior to you based on how you feel about their family, race, socio-economic status or other quality; you will tend to avoid them.

We are all victims of someone's pecking order. But Jesus taught us to remove those barriers. He calls His followers to move beyond comfort-based relationships, to love and serve people who are different from us.

> There is neither Jew nor Gentile, neither slave
> nor free, nor is there male and female, for you
> are all one in Christ Jesus. — **Galatians 3:28**

Now you must figure out how to become a companion to those who are of a different race, gender, class, status or life-stage. You have to bridge the gap toward people to whom you may feel inferior and those to whom you feel superior. As you begin to view *all* people as made in the image of God it will be easier to love the ones who are different from you.

Remember, your identity comes from being a child of God made in His image, and your worth comes from what God has said about you on the cross, nothing more and nothing less. As human beings, we each have the same worth.

1. **Around what types of people are you most comfortable?**

You can benefit from people who are different from you. If you are only around people who are similar to you in age and background, your ability to learn and grow is limited. Although there are appropriate times to learn with people going through similar life circumstances, it is also important to learn from people with different life experiences.

For example, if you struggle with addictions you should learn from people who have overcome addictions—not only speak with people who are still struggling. If you want a better marriage, you should seek out an older couple who has weathered many years together and ask them how they did it—not only speak to your friends who have no more marriage experience than you do.

In other words, you need to learn from people who already are where you want to be. You may believe that you can relate better to the person who is more similar in age or struggle to you, but the truth is that you can learn more from the person who has made healthy choices, not those who are making the same destructive decisions.

> Plans fail for lack of counsel, but with many
> advisers they succeed. —**Proverbs 15:22**

We tend to like people who are similar to us. We establish loyalty to certain "tribes" in the world. We identify with people who share our interests. This can be based on shared ethnicity, cultural background, hobbies, interests, religion or nationality. We tend to view the world through the eyes of our group and often see others as inferior to us.

As citizens of the Kingdom, we no longer value people based on whether or not they fit in our "group" or share our preferences in life. We understand the Jesus' kingdom consists of people from every tribe and group. This loyalty takes precedence over every social group we have formulated in the world. We begin to identify ourselves as children of God and citizens of His Kingdom.

> After this I looked, and there before me was
> a great multitude that no one could count,
> from every nation, tribe, people and language,
> standing before the throne and before the
> Lamb. — **Revelations 7:9a**

When Jesus chose disciples, He picked a radically diverse group.[18] Some were Zealots (patriotic militants); some worked as tax collectors for Israel's national enemy, Rome. There were men and women, rich and poor, educated and uneducated. They travelled and lived together with Jesus for several years. Through interacting with a diverse group of people, Jesus modeled how we can learn and grow through companionship with people who are different from us. Although their backgrounds were different, they shared a new allegiance: loyalty to Jesus.

2. In what ways can you benefit by building
    relationships with people who have different life
    experiences than yours?

3. In what way can the Comfortable Attitude limit or keep
    you from serving others the way Jesus did?

ACTION STEP:

Turn to *Appendix 2* and complete the *Relational Attitude
Assessment*.

List the Relational Attitudes that you exhibit.

developing a healthy relational attitude

Following are steps and actions that will assist you in developing a healthy relational attitude toward others and become a companion—helper—to them.

Know your strengths and your purpose. Be confident in who you are and how God made you.

> I praise you because I am fearfully and
> wonderfully made; your works are wonderful,
> I know that full well. — **Psalm 139:14**

Confidence in your purpose and how God perfectly made you to fulfill it enables you to love people for who they are rather than comparing yourself to them or allowing yourself to be defined by how they treat you.

1. List some strengths God has given you.

Identify your misconceptions and biases toward people. If you are aware of these, you can keep yourself in check and avoid knee-jerk opinions while interacting with others.

> But if we were more discerning with regard
> to ourselves, we would not come under such
> judgment. — **1 Corinthians 11:31**

2. What types of people do you find easy to prejudge?

Always be aware of your mood, emotions and weaknesses. By being aware, you can know that *you* are having a bad day and that other people might not be the problem. You can become aware of what triggers your moods and learn new ways to cope. This can keep you from damaging your relationships. Learn to say, *"Today isn't a good day for me."* Know the point where you need to walk away and cool down. Do not use this as a way to *avoid* necessary interactions, conversations or confrontation, but use it when space is needed. Then go back when your emotions are in check. *1 Corinthians 11:31 (above) also applies here.*

3. Identify strong negative emotions with which you struggle, such as anger, depression, anxiety, and/or irritability. Make note of any triggers you recognize.

Have a strong support team. You need people in your life who encourage you and candidly speak truth to you and about you.

> Wounds from a sincere friend are better than
> many kisses from an enemy.
> — **Proverbs 27:6 NLT**

4. Who are people you allow to speak honestly to you about your weaknesses?

Be able to initiate relationships and find common ground with others. Good companions learn to seek out relationships. They do not just wait for people to come to them and understand them. They go to people and seek to understand others before asking to be understood.[19] Remember, understanding someone's view is not necessarily agreeing with them; it demonstrates respect, which allows you to build a relationship.

> Here is a simple rule of thumb for behavior:
> Ask yourself what you want people to do for
> you; then grab the initiative and do it for them!
> — Luke 6:31 MSG

5. Rate your ability on a scale of 1 to 5 to find common ground with people who are different from you. Explain your rating.

Be able to handle rejection. Learn to love others because of your love for and from God, not because they are lovable or love you in return. Treat them based upon your character (that is, the character of Christ in you), not on their character.

> Blessed are you when people insult you,
> persecute you and falsely say all kinds of evil
> against you because of Me. Rejoice and be glad,
> because great is your reward in heaven, for in
> the same way they persecuted the prophets
> who were before you. — Matthew 5:11-12

6. In what ways do you typically respond to rejection?

Seek ways to serve and love others unconditionally.

> Don't look out only for your own interests, but
> take an interest in others, too.
> — Philippians 2:4 NLT

7. Describe the last time you did something for
    someone without expecting anything, not even
    a thank you, in return.

forgiveness

And forgive us our debts,
as we also have forgiven our
debtors. —MATTHEW 6:12

what is forgiveness?

It is nearly impossible to move forward in building healthy relationships while carrying "baggage" from the past. We must learn how to forgive others for any harm they have inflicted on us and make amends for the harm we have inflicted upon others. Forgiveness may be the most difficult topic to address. We will begin with understanding what forgiveness *is* and what it *is not.* [20]

WHAT IT MEANS TO FORGIVE

To forgive means to *let go of a debt.*[21] It is a decision to stop seeking payback or revenge. Forgiveness is a decision to let it all go.

Forgiveness can be hard because when someone wrongs us, it dishonors and disrespects us on a very fundamental level; it can feel degrading. It can feel as if the other person is positioning themselves as superior to us. This violates our dignity. It violates our humanity. It violates our perceived rights.

THE TRUTH ABOUT FORGIVENESS

Forgiveness is not denying what happened. Denying a hurt does not fix the hurt. Denial can actually deepen the bitterness in your heart. Forgiveness is actually acknowledging that, *Yes, you owe me. You took something from me—emotionally, physically, and/or relationally—but I choose to let go of the debt. I am no longer expecting payback.* The truth is, some things that people have done to you could never be paid back anyway.

Forgiveness is not condoning the action. By forgiving, you are not saying that what was done was okay. You are not dismissing the severity of the actions and you are not giving the person who hurt you permission to do it again.

Forgiveness is not agreeing to trust again. This is probably the biggest hang-up to forgiveness. You may believe that in order to forgive you have to make yourself vulnerable to the offender again. Forgiveness is not the same thing as trust. Forgiveness is *your* responsibility; rebuilding trust is *theirs*. (We will learn more about this in the next section.)

1. Which of these truths about forgiveness stands out to you? Explain:

2. How will accepting the truth about forgiveness help you forgive others?

FORGIVENESS AND TRUST

If forgiveness is erasing a debt that is owed to us, trusting again is being willing to give a "new loan." Forgiveness is the responsibility of the one who has been hurt or is owed. Rebuilding trust is primarily the responsibility of the offender.

For example: Let's say you borrowed $1,000 from a bank. You did not pay it back, but the bank officer chose to forgive or cancel your debt. This means he no longer expects you to pay back what is owed; the bank has absorbed the cost.[22] Just because he forgave you what you owed his bank does not mean he is willing to give you a new loan. Giving a new loan would make him and the bank vulnerable to you again. A new loan depends on your future trustworthiness.

Let's take it a step further: Let's say you work for that bank and stole the $1,000 you needed. The bank officer chose to forgive you of the theft and did not prosecute you. In other words, he did not expect payback or punishment. He absorbed the cost. That is forgiveness and that is *his choice to make*. Expecting him to give you your job back would be expecting him to trust you again. That would depend on you and your demonstrated trustworthiness. Working on your trustworthiness is *your choice to make*.

When someone asks for the chance to rebuild trust they are saying, *"I want to remain in a relationship with you. Give me a chance to make it right and I will show you that I will treat you better."*

Allowing that person to rebuild trust is necessary if you plan to remain in a relationship with them. If you continue to bring up the past and refuse to give them an opportunity to prove that they have changed, a future relationship will be difficult or impossible to maintain. On the other hand, it will be difficult or even unwise to attempt to rebuild a relationship with an offender who shows no remorse for their actions and does not demonstrate change in their character.

3. **Explain the difference between forgiveness and trust.**

If you are trying to rebuild trust with someone, it will take some time. Trust can only be rebuilt by showing consistency over a long period of time. The depth of the relationship and the seriousness of the offense will determine the amount of time it takes to rebuild trust. If the offence is deep, saying "I'm sorry" or "I'll change" is probably not enough to cause the other person to trust you again. What specific steps are you taking to actually work on yourself, your weaknesses and your trustworthiness? Are you seeking Biblical counseling? Are you establishing personal accountability with Godly people? Are you intentionally growing in your relationship with God?

4. If you are trying to rebuild trust, what are some tangible things you can do to demonstrate you can be trusted again?

WHEN DISTANCE IS NECESSARY

> If it is possible, as far as it depends on you, live at peace with everyone. — **Romans 12:18**

Sometimes the only way to live peaceably with someone is by putting distance between them and you. This should usually be a last resort, not a knee-jerk reaction. *Read Matthew 18:15-17.*

If the person who hurt you demonstrates unwillingness to change and continues to harm you, it is scripturally appropriate to end the relationship. This does not mean that you refuse to forgive them; rather, you are putting space between you and them so you can forgive and not remain bitter. *This decision should be reached only after careful prayer and the counsel of a pastor or spiritually mature friend(s).*

You should usually maintain willingness to rebuild the relationship if the person has demonstrated change. However, in some situations, especially those involving violence and sexual abuse, it may never be appropriate to re-enter the relationship no matter how much change the offender has demonstrated. Again, seek the guidance of a pastor or spiritually mature friend.

5. What does it mean to forgive someone and not re-enter a relationship with them?

why should I forgive?

Read Matthew 18:21-35

You forgive because you have been forgiven. In this story, Jesus illustrates how we owe God a huge debt, but He chose to forgive us. In order for you to be able to forgive, it is important that you have first received forgiveness. It is difficult to give others what you have not received. The Bible teaches that if we confess our sins God will forgive us.

> If we confess our sins, he is faithful and just and will forgive us our sins and purify us from all unrighteousness. — **1 John 1:9**

The Bible also teaches that God forgives because of Who He is—love—not because we are worthy of forgiveness.

> But God demonstrates his own love for us in this: While we were still sinners, Christ died for us. — **Romans 5:8**

1. **If you have not received God's forgiveness, pause and ask Him for it. If you have received His forgiveness, pause and thank Him for it.**

God freely extends forgiveness to you, then asks you to extend it to others. Jesus went as far as to say that if you do not forgive others, God will not forgive you.

> But if you do not forgive others their sins, your
> Father will not forgive your sins.
> — Matthew 6:15

To be clear, forgiving others is not some action or work that we do in order to earn our own forgiveness. Refusal to forgive demonstrates the unchanged condition of our own heart. Remember that when we are saved, the Holy Spirit—the Spirit of Jesus— enters into us and changes us. Jesus is actually living in us, enabling us to do the impossible. Jesus has forgiven us of our debt toward God and then empowers us to forgive others of what they owe us.

> My old self has been crucified with Christ. It is
> no longer I who live, but Christ lives in me. So
> I live in this earthly body by trusting in the Son
> of God, who loved me and gave himself for me.
> — Galatians 2:20 NLT

So yes, when someone takes from you or hurts you, it is an insult to your humanity. It disrespects you and dishonors you. Forgiving them can seem to violate your perceived rights, but never forget you were crucified with Christ. You are now dead. But Christ lives through you. In your own power, forgiveness might seem impossible; but through Christ all things are possible.

A final reminder: As a child of God, forgiveness is never optional, but trust does not have to be automatic. Whether or not you trust the other person again depends upon *their* actions; but forgiveness is about *your* actions before God. When God tells you to forgive, He is not asking you to deny or condone what others did to you. He is not even asking you to trust people who have hurt you. He is simply asking you to extend the same grace to others that has been given to you.

2. How does the realization that you have been forgiven by God and empowered by the Holy Spirit help you forgive others?

Forgiveness frees you. Notice that at the end of Jesus' story, the unforgiving person is handed over to tormentors. Refusing to forgive enslaves you. The offense then torments you and will destroy your life. It tells you when to sleep and when to wake up. It tells you where you can go and how you get to feel. By telling you to forgive, God is saving you from the torment of the offense and the bitterness it produces.

The process of forgiving can be painful. Depending on the seriousness of the offense, forgiving may feel like death inside. This is true because when you forgive, you are absorbing the damages done to you. You no longer seek repayment, revenge or restitution from the one who harmed you. (Remember the bank examples from the previous lesson.) Forgiveness is emotionally hard, but on the other side the freedom from anger and bitterness is a harvest worth the price.

It has been said that holding on to unforgiveness is like drinking poison and expecting the other person to die or holding fire in your hand and expecting the other person to get burned. *Let it go.* Your offender might not deserve better, but you do. Remember that Jesus came to give you life. When He tells you to forgive, or anything else for that matter, it is to help you truly live (John 6:68).

3. In what ways has unforgiveness robbed you of life and kept you in torment?

Forgiveness leaves room for God. In other words, let God settle the score. In its basic form, taking revenge is playing God. Revenge is about being in control. Punishing the wicked is God's business, not ours. When you seek revenge, you are saying that you do not trust God's ability to handle the situation. Scripture teaches that God will either change the person or He will settle the score.

> Do not take revenge, my dear friends, but leave room for God's wrath, for it is written: "It is mine to avenge; I will repay," says the Lord.
> — **Romans 12:19**

> "As surely as I live," says the Sovereign LORD, "I take no pleasure in the death of wicked people. I only want them to turn from their wicked ways so they can live. Turn! Turn from your wickedness, O people of Israel! Why should you die?" — **Ezekiel 33:11 NLT**

4. **Why is it difficult to trust God to settle the score with others?**

the step beyond forgiveness

We have been learning the importance of choosing to forgive, but Jesus also teaches us to go a step *beyond* forgiveness.

Read Luke 6:27-36.

This passage of Scripture brings up a couple of questions: Why would Jesus teach us to do good to people who have hurt us? Forgiving them and letting go of the offense can be hard enough— why should we do more?

FIGHTING AGAINST OUR REAL ENEMY

The Bible teaches that people are not your enemy. We must remember that our real enemy is Satan.

> For our struggle is *not against flesh and blood,*
> but against the rulers, against the authorities,
> against the powers of this dark world and
> against the spiritual forces of evil in the
> heavenly realms.
> — **Ephesians 6:12** *(Emphasis added)*

It is difficult to understand and accept that your enemies are victims of the same evil that you are susceptible to. Satan not only uses them to hurt you, he also destroys them in the process.

When you choose to pray for them, you begin to fight a war against the real evil in the world. You release God's power to work to change those who have harmed you, not just punish them. This is in no way condoning what they did, because each person is responsible for the choices they make. However, praying for those who have hurt you is your choice to wage war against the true enemy—Satan.

1. How does choosing to pray for those who have hurt you impact the way you view them?

OVERCOME EVIL WITH GOOD

Sometimes the act of repaying evil with good will actually convict the person of the evil they are doing and cause them to change.

> Do not repay anyone evil for evil. Be careful to do what is right in the eyes of everyone… On the contrary: "If your enemy is hungry, feed him; if he is thirsty, give him something to drink. In doing this, you will heap burning coals on his head." Do not be overcome by evil, but overcome evil with good.
> — Romans 12:17, 20-21

Notice the last part of the previous Scripture passage: *overcome evil with good*. The word *overcome* denotes action. Repaying evil with good denotes a deliberate action to work against evil by doing something good.

Satan's goal is destruction. He seeks to divide and destroy us. When you repay evil with good, you stop Satan's ongoing work of destruction in the world. But when you repay evil with evil, you continue Satan's work.

The greatest threat to you is not the act that was done to you; the greatest threat to you is the after-effects of bitterness and revenge. Bitterness and revenge can eventually turn you into the same type of person who hurt you.

Hatred and revenge are natural reactions of our old human nature (Galatians 5:19-21). Yet God seeks to create the person of Christ in you. That new person is full of love, joy, peace, patience, kindness, goodness, faithfulness, gentleness and self-control (Galatians 5:22-23).

When you choose to bless rather than curse, when you choose to pray rather than seek revenge, when you choose to repay an evil act with a good act, you limit the spread of evil. You destroy Satan's work in the world.

You actually *overcome* evil with good. You cannot change what someone did to you, but you can counteract the effects of it by doing a good act for every evil act done to you. By doing good, you cancel out the effect of that evil act in the world.

Many times — after using their pain to help others — people find a way to make sense of their pain.

NOTE: Sometimes it is unwise to be around the person who has hurt you or whom you have hurt. You may be legally restrained from them, or you may put your life in jeopardy by being around them. In those instances, you can still keep your heart pure and pray for them and pray that God frees them from the evil that has them bound. You may not actually be the one who brings help to them, but you can pray for God to bring it through someone else. You can counteract their evil by doing good to another victim of a similar offense.

2. What is your reaction to the concept of cancelling out evil with good? Explain:

DAY 16

make an amends list

The fact that we all live in a world of sin means that *people have hurt us and that we have hurt people.* Surrendering to Christ does not mean that all the past issues in your life are automatically resolved. Many people carry around emotional "baggage" for years. It slows down their spiritual journey, hurts their relationship with God and keeps them from enjoying healthy companionship with others.

It is important to start with a clean slate and go forward. Creating a clean slate requires asking forgiveness from people whom you have hurt and also telling people that you have forgiven them. [23]

> Therefore, since we are surrounded by such a huge crowd of witnesses to the life of faith, let us *strip off every weight that slows us down,* especially the sin that so easily trips us up. And let us run with endurance the race God has set before us.
> — **Hebrews 12:1 NLT** *(Emphasis added)*

> I press on to possess that perfection for which Christ Jesus first possessed me. No, dear brothers and sisters, I have not achieved it, but I focus on this one thing: *Forgetting the past and looking forward to what lies ahead,* I press on to reach the end of the race.
> — **Philippians 3:12b-14a NLT** *(Emphasis added)*

If God has forgiven you, you should receive His forgiveness and not live in guilt anymore.

> Therefore, there is now no condemnation for
> those who are in Christ Jesus. — **Romans 8:1**

As much as possible, you should make amends with people whom you have hurt as well as with those who have hurt you.

MAKING AN AMENDS LIST

In separate notebook begin making your *Amends List*. Keep this list in a safe place. Following are several areas to think through and consider as you make your list:

Review the *Personal Sin Inventory* you completed in *Book 2: Discover Freedom.* When you completed this inventory, you identified people who have hurt you and people whom you have hurt. This is a good place to start compiling your *Amends List*.

- Look through the list and identify people *who have hurt you* by committing any sins against you (people who lied to you; people who stole from you; people who abused you or mistreated you, etc.).

- As you go through the list, think about whom *you have hurt* by committing sins against them (people you lied to; people you stole from; people you betrayed, etc.).

- Think about whom *you have sinned with*. If possible, you should let them know you have changed and apologize to them for involving them in your sin (people you should not have had sex with; people you abused drugs with; people you stole with, etc.).

Categories of People to Consider: As you make your list, there are different people you should think about. Did they hurt you, did you hurt them, did you sin with them?

- Parents or guardians

- Current or former spouse

- Current or former girlfriend/boyfriend

- Your children

- Your siblings

- Your extended family (grandparents, aunts, uncles, cousins)

- Teachers

- Classmates

- Current or former boss

- Current or former coworkers

- Current or former neighbors

- Current or former friends

Be sure to go back to your earliest memories. Childhood experiences can shape the rest of our lives. Don't forget to consider all childhood influences such as friends, parents, teachers, boyfriends, girlfriends, etc.

Ask the Holy Spirit to reveal any area you may have overlooked (Psalm 139:23-24).

1. **Identify and discuss any questions you have concerning making an *Amends List*.**

Note: Be prepared to talk about your progress on your list in your next group meeting. You do not have to share details with everyone, just how you are progressing.

make amends

After you have made your list:

Ask God to forgive you of your sins. We have all hurt God, others, and ourselves. We should receive His forgiveness.

Remind yourself the past is gone! It is normal for thoughts from the past to return. Memories of pain or thoughts of revenge or guilt may resurface without warning or reason. Take control of the inner dialogue in your mind and remind yourself that the past is gone.

> Therefore if any man be in Christ, he is a new creature: old things are passed away; behold, all things are become new.
> — II Corinthians 5:17 AKJV

After each entry on your list, identify how you can attempt to make amends. Making amends means that you ASK people whom you have hurt to forgive you; and it means that you TELL others that you have forgiven them. Review the *tips for making amends* section that follows.

Consider how you can "cancel out" the evil with good. Review *Day 15: The Step Beyond Forgiveness.* Ask God to create opportunities for you to do good to the people who have hurt you, or to show you how to help others who have been similarly hurt. Prayerfully consider and list a response to each hurt you have endured.

Set a time to prayerfully go through your list with a trusted accountability partner.

1. When will this time be?

Go make amends when possible. You will be amazed at the freedom you discover when you take this huge step of forgiveness in your life. The process may be uncomfortable, but the payoff is HUGE.

> No discipline seems pleasant at the time,
> but painful. Later on, however, it produces a
> harvest of righteousness and peace for those
> who have been trained by it. — **Hebrews 12:11**

IMPORTANT TIPS FOR MAKING AMENDS

Sometimes people WILL NOT FORGIVE YOU when you ask.
If this happens, do your part, which is to ask for forgiveness, then move forward. Do not make excuses for your actions; simply tell the person that you know that you hurt them and apologize.

Sometimes people WILL NOT ADMIT they have wronged you.
When you tell people that you have forgiven them for hurting you, they may become combative and try to argue or justify their behavior. Do not argue with them or try to convince them of their wrongdoing. Just do your part, which is to forgive, then move forward.

Sometimes you SHOULD NOT contact the person or address the situation. If initiating contact will hurt that person, yourself or others, you should not attempt to make amends. But beware: it is easy to use this as an excuse to never attempt to make amends. If in doubt, seek advice from a pastor or other mature Christian you trust.

Sometimes you CANNOT contact the person. There may be legal or physical barriers between you and the other person, or they may be deceased.

If you should not or cannot contact them, a symbolic action such as writing a letter and then destroying it or visiting a grave to make peace can be liberating.

> If it is possible, *as far as it depends on you,* live at peace with everyone. — **Romans 12:18**
> *(Emphasis added)*

2. Identify and discuss any questions you have concerning making amends.

NOTE: Be prepared to talk about your progress on your list in your next group meeting. You do not have to share details with everyone, just how you are progressing.

conflict resolution

If it is possible, as far as it depends on you, live at peace with everyone. — ROMANS 12:18

resolving conflict

While it is important to clean up our past relational failures and conflicts, it is also important to allow Jesus' teaching to guide how we handle future conflicts.

When you have a relationship with someone, the question is not, "What will I do *if* we have a conflict?" The question is, "What will I do *when* we have a conflict?" The inability to appropriately handle conflicts robs many of us of meaningful relationships.

All relationships go through conflict. Unfortunately, church families are not immune to conflicts. Satan most actively tries to destroy church relationships because when people in churches are unified, people see Jesus in us, and lives are changed.

> I in them and you in me—so that they may be brought to complete unity. Then the world will know that you sent me and have loved them even as you have loved me. — **John 17:23**

Many of us were not taught how to handle problems in God-honoring ways. One benefit of being in God's family is that you can learn healthy things that you did not learn in your natural family. However, as adults our old patterns of behavior are deeply engrained. *It will take time and uncomfortable situations to change the way you handle conflict.*

COMMON APPROACHES TO HANDLING CONFLICT

Attacking. If you respond to conflict by attacking, you rely on fear and intimidation to force your own way during a disagreement. To overcome this habit, remember that the goal of conflict resolution is not to win or be right; it is to find a solution that respects both parties. Remember that honesty, while it might be painful, does not have to be aggressive.

> Do nothing out of selfish ambition or vain conceit. Rather, in humility value others above yourselves, not looking to your own interests but each of you *to the interests of the others*.
> — **Philippians 2:3-4** *(Emphasis added)*

Manipulating. If you manipulate to get your way during a conflict, you most likely pout and/or use guilt, or play on emotions in other ways. You are not necessarily confrontational or aggressive but are sneakier in your approach. You are likely dishonest about your true feelings. You may say what you think others want to hear, then leave and do what you want. Jesus insists that we are to be honest with our feelings. Being honest does not mean you are being "ugly."

RULE OF THUMB: Learn to say what you mean and mean what you say.

> All you need to say is simply "Yes" or "No"; anything beyond this comes from the evil one.
> — **Matthew 5:37**

Ignoring. To ignore a problem is to pretend that it does not exist. If you take this approach, you "hide your head in the sand." You downplay and ignore serious issues. Although it is true that we should not overreact, pretending that problems do not exist only compounds them.

> They dress the wound of my people as though
> it were not serious. "Peace, peace," they say,
> when there is no peace. — **Jeremiah 6:14**

Running. If you take this approach, you run from a relationship when there is a conflict. Rather than enduring the discomfort of seeking a resolution, you abandon the relationship. Jesus insists that you do your part to work out your conflicts and not avoid them.

> Therefore, if you are offering your gift at the
> altar and there remember that your brother or
> sister has something against you, leave your
> gift there in front of the altar. First go and be
> reconciled to them; then come and offer your
> gift. — **Matthew 5:23-24**

Silence. When you take this approach, you refuse to talk about the problem. It's not that you necessarily deny conflicts or leave the relationship—you simply will not talk about it.

> If your brother or sister sins, go and point out
> their fault, just between the two of you. If they
> listen to you, you have won them over.
> — **Matthew 18:15**

1. **Which of these five is the most natural or common for you to respond with?**

2. Write out the verses that challenge your common approach and place them in places around your home and/or work for you to consistently see. This will help reshape your approach to conflict resolution.

3. Think about the last conflict (big or small) that you had with someone. Did you respond with one of these five approaches? If yes, which one? If no, in what way(s) did you handle it?

biblical conflict resolution

THE "MATTHEW 18 PRINCIPLE" FOR CONFLICT RESOLUTION

> If your brother or sister sins, go and point out their fault, just between the two of you. If they listen to you, you have won them over. But if they will not listen, take one or two others along, so that "every matter may be established by the testimony of two or three witnesses." If they still refuse to listen, tell it to the church; and if they refuse to listen even to the church, treat them as you would a pagan or a tax collector. — **Matthew 18:15-17**

1. **List the four steps from this passage that Jesus taught to resolve conflict.**

2. Is there currently an unresolved conflict with someone in your life? If so, what is the next step you need to take according to Matthew 18:15-17?

THREE TYPES OF PEOPLE YOU INTERACT WITH

In their book, *Boundaries,* Cloud and Townsend describe three categories of people with whom we have conflict.[24] These categories are based on the following Bible passage:

> Leave your simple ways and you will live;
> walk in the way of insight. Whoever corrects
> a mocker invites insults; whoever rebukes the
> wicked incurs abuse. Do not rebuke mockers
> or they will hate you; rebuke the wise and they
> will love you. — **Proverbs 9:6-8**

This passage tells us that some people are wise, some are mockers—which means they are foolish—and some are wicked. You cannot deal with all three groups in the same ways.

Talk it out with wise people. Wise in this context does not refer to a person's intellect, but rather to their ability to take advice and make good decisions. A wise person will listen and make changes when you speak with them.

Note that sometimes a personality conflict inhibits people from being able to talk though their problems together. If this is the case, the problem may not be that the person does not want to listen or change, they may not understand you. This is why Jesus said that if you cannot get a problem worked out one-on-one, take someone else along. A mediator can help clarify issues.

Enforce consequences for foolish people. If you keep talking to someone and there is no change, you are probably dealing with a foolish person. A foolish person needs to feel consequences before they change.

Warn them of the consequences, and if they still do not listen, simply stop trying to convince them and begin enforcing the previously stated consequence or allow them to experience the natural consequences of their behavior. When this happens, the foolish person may choose to change or may choose to become angry and stay away from you.

Place boundaries between yourself and wicked people. Some people are toxic and want to hurt you. You should do your best to limit all contact with them.

Not every person who disagrees with you is toxic. When a foolish person cannot get their way with you and refuses to change, they usually just get mad and leave you alone, or will continue to argue with you, if you allow it. A toxic person, however, will try to hurt you. They will try to inflict physical, legal, financial or relational pain on you. This is the type of person Paul describes when he tells Titus to warn them twice and then have nothing more to do with them.

> Warn a divisive person once, and then warn them a second time. After that, have nothing to do with them. — **Titus 3:10**

3. **Identify people with whom you have had conflict, that may fall into each of these categories.**

    Wise:

    Foolish:

    Wicked:

4. Describe the different ways to interact with each group of people:

Wise:

Foolish:

Wicked:

DAY 20

reacting to injustice

There are times when we are treated unjustly and cannot find a resolution. Not all relationships can be restored, and we cannot remove ourselves completely from all unrepentant, toxic offenders. For example, people in power may abuse their authority or a family member might treat you unfairly.

Read Matthew 5:38-42

Through this teaching, Jesus tells us to think of ways that expose injustice without resorting to violence or giving in to timidity. He teaches us a third way.[25] Understanding the Jewish custom of Jesus' day will shed some light on the meaning of His teaching in this passage.

If anyone slaps you on the right cheek, turn to them the other cheek also. In order for someone to hit you on the right cheek, they must either use their *left* hand or *backhand* you with their right. (Go ahead and take a minute to figure this out in your mind.) Both actions were degrading acts, intended to insult the person being hit.

It was considered a degrading insult to hit someone by using your left hand. Some communities would actually punish people for hitting someone with their left hand. The left hand was reserved for "unclean" acts.

A backhand is also a very degrading hit used on someone who is considered your inferior to put them in their place. For example, how an abusive husband would hit his wife or a master would hit a slave.

The point is, hitting someone on the right cheek was a degrading act. So, if someone hits you on your right cheek and you offer them your left cheek, you are forcing the abuser to look at you and hit you with their right hand and thus you choose to preserve your dignity, even if they do not recognize it. (Again, take a minute to think through this.) We might not be able to stop abuse, but we do not have to allow an abuser to strip the dignity of the image of God from us.

1. What stands out to you about this concept? Explain:

If anyone wants to sue you and take your coat, hand over your shirt as well. In this culture, the poor could easily be taken into court and sued for the only thing they had left —even the coat on their backs. Wealthy landlords would often do this.

Jesus taught that when someone wrongfully takes some of your clothes, strip all of your clothes off and give them everything you have as well. Being naked was very shameful in that culture. *Causing* someone to be naked was considered even more shameful.

By stripping down and exposing yourself to the world, you bring shame and expose the unjust actions of your oppressors.

2. What stands out to you about this concept? Explain:

If anyone forces you to go one mile, go with them two miles.
In this culture, a Roman soldier—the Jewish oppressors—could force anyone to carry their belongings for a mile. To force them to go a second mile was not allowed and was actually an infraction of military code. To see a Jewish person walking two miles with a soldier could suggest friendship.

By teaching us to go an extra mile, Jesus taught us that we still have a choice, even if someone can force us to do something against our will. The second mile is our decision. The second mile shows them the serving attitude of Jesus.

3. **What stands out to you about this concept? Explain:**

The point of this teaching goes beyond the three examples that Jesus gives. In all three of these scenarios, Jesus taught us how to creatively resist evil. He taught us to stand and react in a third way that goes against the natural tendencies of *flight* or *fight*. We can stand and maintain dignity, even when abused; we can stand and expose the shame of unfair treatment; we can stand and serve our enemies, even more than they can force us to. By doing so, we actively resist and expose evil with good.

4. **Identify some examples in history when people have applied these creative acts of resistance to expose unfair and evil abuses of power.**

5. Does this teaching from Jesus make you uncomfortable? Explain:

6. How can you apply Jesus' third way to creatively settle an injustice you may be suffering?

DAY 21
avoiding gossip

It is difficult to talk about Godly conflict resolution and communication without dealing with the issue of gossip. For the purpose of today, gossip will be defined as *discussing someone else's business in a negative way.*

Rather than talking *to* people about issues, we often talk *about* them.

Gossip *destroys* safety and relationships. We cannot become the family that God wants us to be and show love to the world around us if we are gossipers. Gossiping makes you a *dangerous* person to be around. Notice what the Bible says about gossip:

> Do not go about spreading slander among your people. Do not do anything that endangers your neighbor's life. I am the Lord.
> — **Leviticus 19:16**

> A gossip betrays a confidence; so avoid anyone who talks too much. —**Proverbs 20:19**

> Without wood a fire goes out; without a gossip a quarrel dies down. — **Proverbs 26:20**

> There are six things the Lord hates, seven that are detestable to him: haughty eyes, a lying tongue, hands that shed innocent blood, a heart that devises wicked schemes, feet that are quick to rush into evil, a false witness who pours out lies and *a person who stirs up conflict in the community.* — **Proverbs 6:16-19** *(Emphasis added)*

As you truly find your security, worth and satisfaction in Christ, you become less and less interested in other people's opinions and problems. Rather than wanting to discuss others' problems, you are motivated to be a companion and help them. You are motivated to talk *to* them, not *about* them.

GOSSIP MOTIVES

Gossip is actually passing judgment behind someone's back. Pointing out other people's mistakes and shortcomings can make you feel better about yourself. However, cutting other people down does not elevate you. Christ has already raised you up to Heavenly places with Him. Remember that you are a child of God made in His image; that should be enough to define you.

You may use gossip in order to validate your worth by comparing yourself to others and deciding that your life, actions and morality are superior. If you receive your worth from Jesus, you no longer need to compare your life with others to feel your worth. You are content with God's approval.

Gossip can feel fulfilling. You develop an appetite or "need" to know other people's problems. Sometimes being the first to know something can give you a sense of accomplishment or satisfaction. You can also feel validated by getting sympathy from people by sharing what someone else has done to you. However, the more you are fulfilled by a relationship with God, the less you will need to feed off of other people's problems or opinions.

1. Think carefully about the last time you discussed someone else's business. List the "benefit" you received in the conversation. Keep in mind the truth that we always do things for a reason — often an unconscious one.

THREE GOSSIP MYTHS

If I repeat it just once, it won't matter. It is gossip *every time* you talk about someone else's business in a negative way.

If I'm only listening, it's not gossip. Unless you are mediating or intervening, you are participating in gossip by *listening* to someone discuss someone else's business in a negative way.

If I'm telling the truth it is not gossip. Gossip is telling what you *think is the truth*. Slander is intentionally telling a lie. Both are sin.

At times, you may find it necessary to involve someone else in a problem. It is not gossip if the two of you are working out a solution to resolve the problem or are planning how to intervene and help to restore a fallen brother or sister. But BEWARE: often what is passed off as seeking help is really seeking sympathy or looking for someone else who enjoys discussing other people's problems.

RULE OF THUMB: If you are not part of the problem and not part of the solution, stay out of it.

Unless you are seeking help or are planning to mediate or intervene, you should not talk about it.

2. List an example of how you can talk about another person's problem with others, in order to find a solution or intervene. How does this differ from gossiping?

3. Ask the Holy Spirit to convict and redirect you every time you engage in a gossiping conversation.

tips for healthy conflict resolution

Make allowances for people. Maybe they are just having a bad day. Be willing to let the offense go.

> Always be humble and gentle. Be patient with each other, making allowance for each other's faults because of your love.
> — **Ephesians 4:2 NLT**

Take care of problems quickly. If you cannot let it go, take care of it quickly. The longer it goes, the bigger it becomes.

> In your anger do not sin: Do not let the sun go down while you are still angry.
> — **Ephesians 4:26**

Talk to people, not about them. If someone has hurt you or if you are worried about sinful behavior in their life, you should talk to them, not about them.

> If your brother or sister sins, go and point out their fault, just between the two of you. If they listen to you, you have won them over.
> — **Matthew 18:15**

Keep your tone and emotions in check. Even if you are angry you must watch how you express yourself. Remember Ephesians 4:26: *In your anger do not sin.*

> A gentle answer turns away wrath, but a harsh word stirs up anger. — **Proverbs 15:1**

Speak candidly, but avoid escalating, belittling or name-calling.[26] Be honest about how someone makes you feel with their actions, but do not treat them like they are less than you.

> Do not let any unwholesome talk come out
> of your mouths, but only what is helpful for
> building others up according to their needs,
> that it may benefit those who listen.
> — Ephesians 4:29

Do not assume or accuse—ask.[27] If you wonder what a person meant by a certain action or words, *ask* them. Focus on explaining how those things made you feel, then ask if that was their intention. Example: *Did you intend to embarrass me when you did that?* Rather than: *You're always trying to embarrass me!*

> Fools have no interest in understanding; they
> only want to air their own opinions.
> — Proverbs 18:2 NLT

Listen and clarify before you reply.[28] Speak one at a time and do not interrupt. Often, we do not listen with the intent of understanding but with the intent of replying.

Clarify by repeating back what you heard the other person say. We all can misunderstand what someone else is saying, and it is helpful when people hear their concerns are understood.

Even if you do not agree, listening and clarifying show the other person that you consider them valuable and are listening.

If you are mediating a conflict, do not allow people to interrupt each other. Insist that they speak one at a time, and carefully clarify before moving forward.

> My dear brothers and sisters, take note of this:
> Everyone should be quick to listen, slow to
> speak and slow to become angry. — James 1:19

> There is more hope for a fool than for someone
> who speaks without thinking.
> — Proverbs 29:20 NLT

Value the relationship more than you value winning the argument. You may not agree with the other person about the matter at hand, but ask yourself, *"Is it really worth losing a relationship over?"*

> Make every effort to keep the unity of the Spirit through the bond of peace. — **Ephesians 4:3**

If you cannot reach an agreement, bring in a mediator. This can be a trusted friend, a counselor or church leader.

> But if they will not listen, take one or two others along, so that "every matter may be established by the testimony of two or three witnesses."
> — **Matthew 18:16**

Be willing to forgive and not carry a grudge. Forgiveness is required. You must not hold a past offense over someone's head; however, trust may have to be earned again.

> Get rid of all bitterness, rage and anger, brawling and slander, along with every form of malice. Be kind and compassionate to one another, forgiving each other, just as in Christ God forgave you. — **Ephesians 4:31-32**

1. Go back and identify any of these areas in which you struggle when it comes to having healthy conflict resolution.

ACTION STEP: A RELATIONAL AGREEMENT

Consider making relational agreements with the people you care about. This can be done with your family, spouse, friends, co-workers or anyone else with whom you have relationships.

The *Relational Agreement* in Appendix 3 is designed to help you commit to implementing what you have been learning.

To download a printable copy of this agreement, visit the *Additional Resources* page of **www.discoverdiscipleship.com.**

the family of God

Consequently, you are
no longer foreigners and
strangers, but fellow citizens
with God's people and also
members of his household.
—EPHESIANS 2:19

the church—God's family

1. When you hear the word "church," what comes to mind?

Church is more than a building, a gathering of people or an organization. The church is God's family. When you are reborn as a child of God, you become part of His family the Church.

> So now you Gentiles are no longer strangers
> and foreigners. You are citizens along with all
> of God's holy people. You are members of God's
> family. — **Ephesians 2:19 NLT**

The family of God is not a metaphor. During the time that Scripture was written, people were often ostracized from their own families and communities when they began to follow Jesus. The church would literally become their new physical family and support system. This is also true for many Christians in different parts of the world today.

Even if we are able to retain our natural family, the church still becomes our new spiritual family. In God's family we get spiritual support and oversight as we grow as His child. Even as a baby needs the loving care of a family, so every child of God needs the support and care of God's family.

Remember, like a lion stalking prey, Satan waits for you to become isolated and alone, and then jumps in for the kill. Do not be ignorant of his tricks. Build strong relationships with safe people.

> Be alert and of sober mind. Your enemy the
> devil prowls around like a roaring lion looking
> for someone to devour. — I Peter 5:8

Many people pursue a relationship with God outside of the contexts of a spiritual church family. Being isolated from other believers is not God's purpose and plan for you as His child. He desires a family with which to share Himself with. Remember God created us for companionship.

Christians should reflect the intent and will of God in the world. We should model and reflect our created design as God's children. This includes loving God and partnering with Him, but it also includes doing so *with* others (*Review Day 2: Unity Lost and Restored* and *Day 3: How to Love Others*).

Even Jesus reflected this by gathering a group of 70 people with whom to share life and ministry with. And then within this group He was more personally connected with the 12 Apostles, most specifically with Peter, James and John.[29]

When we read Scripture, we learn how the first Christians seemed intent on being a family. We learn that although this group had their problems, they knew that church was more than a meeting or a place. Church was *people;* people who shared their lives as friends and family. They began recapturing the common unity that was lost when Adam and Eve sinned.

Notice how this first group of Christians lived and interacted with each other:

Read Acts 2:42-47.

2. What are some distinguishing characteristics of how the first Christians interacted with each other?

3. In what ways do these differ from your experience with church?

BECOMING PART OF A SPIRITUAL FAMILY

When you gave your life to Jesus, you were born into God's family as His child. He now expects you to become an active part of His family by connecting to a local church.

Being part of a spiritual family is about more than meetings — it is about building relationships like the early church did. Simply attending worship services on Sunday does not mean that you are an active part of a spiritual family. Think about your natural family; a healthy family grows stronger by sharing life and responsibility.

4. What does it mean to share life and responsibility?

During public services, the people who make up the church come together as one large family to worship God and celebrate, and to learn from the church's leaders. This can be a great time of unity, inspiration and celebration. However, more is necessary to truly grow as a strong disciple of Jesus and connect with His family.

In order to be an active part of a spiritual family, you need to find people with whom you can intentionally go deeper in life and faith. You need to find people with whom to build relationships and with whom you can intentionally share life (Reference Acts 2:42-47).

One of the best ways to encourage and foster deeper relationships and companionship within a church is through smaller groups of people who meet together for support, spiritual growth and service. We will discuss this in more detail in the next lesson.

This model of meeting together in smaller groups–homes–and gathering for larger public meetings can be found throughout the New Testament. Meeting in homes denotes friendship and more personal spiritual gatherings.

> Every day they continued to meet together in the temple courts. They broke bread in their homes and ate together with glad and sincere hearts. — **Acts 2:46**

> You know that I have not hesitated to preach anything that would be helpful to you but have taught you publicly and from house to house. — **Acts 20:20**

5. **Are you truly an active part of a spiritual family if you do not take time to connect with people on a relational level? Why or why not?**

6. What ways does your church provide for people to connect with others outside of weekly worship services?

7. Are you connected to your church family outside of public worship services? Why or why not?

DAY	
24	

spiritual growth environments

This *Discover Discipleship Course* emphasizes that the life of a disciple is a life of training. Let's review how people typically learn new skills. True mastery of any subject comes through a combination of three learning environments:[30]

LEARNING ENVIRONMENTS

Immersive or Cultural Learning. This refers to people you are around and the natural environment you live in. For example, this is how you learned your first language; you learned it informally by being in a culture that spoke it. This is also the best way to learn a second language—be in a culture that speaks it.

In *Workbook 2: Discover Freedom* we explored how much we learn from the unconscious input of the environment around us. For example, as a child learning to speak, we would listen to people say words in reference to certain objects and then we repeated the words. We desired a result—food. We would hear people reference obtaining food as—"eat." We would say "eat" and the use of the word would be reinforced by someone giving us food. (Typically, after they clapped and celebrated the new word we learned!)

Instructional Learning. This is the learning environment that we normally think of. It is structured, classroom learning. In this environment, information is imparted to us by a teacher.

When we went to school and learned the structure and grammar of our language, our command of that language grew to a new level. We learned new words and learned how to read, which opened up tens of thousands of new words to us. We learned how words work together—grammar. This built on what our culture had informally taught us. The culture you live in has the most impact on your language skills. Instructional learning then takes it to a deeper level.

Coached Learning. When you are coached, someone gives you accountability and personal feedback on your implementation. Coaching helps produce mastery. Sometimes coaching happens informally, as people give you real-time feedback on your performance.

Think about the example of learning a language. When you first began speaking words, you did not always say them correctly. People would give you real-time feedback and correct you, saying the word as it should be pronounced. When you said it correctly, they would reinforce its use by celebrating and/or giving you what you requested.

Coaching can come formally as well. For example, a speaking coach or writing coach can help you break bad habits and take your command of language to a new level. Formal coaching is often necessary because the culture we live in continually reinforces the "bad' habits we have developed.

DISCIPLESHIP ENVIRONMENTS

Using the metaphor of learning a new language, we would say, *"Discipleship is the language of Christians."*

The Immersive or Cultural Component of Discipleship. The people you choose to surround yourself with will make the biggest impact upon your spiritual development. You will learn countless truths through observing and interacting with other believers.

This is why you should become an active part of an extended spiritual church family. This involves more than attending worship services with other believers. It means building friendships and "doing life" with others. These are people you will laugh with, cry with, and serve with.

Having an extended spiritual family of roughly 50-70 other believers in your life will prove to be vitally important to your spiritual development. If your church family is more than 50-70 people—which a growing, healthy church typically is—you will need to find a way to connect with a smaller group of believers in that church family. It can be difficult to be involved in the lives of more than 50 other people, but a network of fewer people can be insufficient.[31]

Churches express this in many ways. This is often expressed through demographic focused ministries such as men's ministries, women's ministries and youth ministries; it can be through community serving ministries or through missional communities. The point is, these are opportunities to be around other believers, in ministry and life contexts, outside of instructional environments. This is also different from small group settings, as we will learn below.

Jesus demonstrated this principle building a culture of at least 72 disciples that often traveled with Him. He did not just preach to the crowds; He developed a traveling community that actually traveled and ministered together. This provided His first disciples the opportunity to learn how to live out the principles of life and ministry He was teaching them.

> After this the Lord appointed seventy-two others
> and sent them two by two ahead of him to every
> town and place where he was about to go.
> — Luke 10:1

> After this, Jesus traveled about from one town
> and village to another, proclaiming the good
> news of the kingdom of God. The Twelve were
> with him, and also some women who had
> been cured of evil spirits and diseases: Mary
> (called Magdalene) from whom seven demons
> had come out; Joanna the wife of Chuza, the
> manager of Herod's household; Susanna; and
> many others. These women were helping to
> support them out of their own means.
> — Luke 8:1-3

The early church also modeled this relational life together. (Acts 2:42-47)

The Instructional Learning Component of Discipleship. It is important to receive regular Bible instruction from gifted Bible teachers and preachers. This is why involvement with a church family's worship gatherings should be a high priority.

Note that instructional learning through preaching and teaching will not take the place of the other two learning environments. However, it is an integral part of your spiritual development.

Jesus and the Apostles demonstrated the value of this by regularly teaching large crowds of people.

> When Jesus landed and saw a large crowd, he had compassion on them, because they were like sheep without a shepherd. So he began teaching them many things. — **Mark 6:34**

The Coaching Component of Discipleship. It is vitally important to have a few spiritually mature people in your life, who will give personal feedback and instruction as you learn to be a disciple of Jesus.

As important as instructional Bible teaching and preaching is, it cannot take the place of personal coaching. A pastor or teacher at the front of a room cannot give you the kind of "life on life" feedback and coaching you need.

Churches often express this through small groups and/or accountability groups. These are often within the context of a larger ministry in the church or can stand alone. The goal is for the group to be small enough for you to build a more personal relationship with a few people. You are more likely to build trust and be more transparent with a smaller group of people, than with a larger group.

This differs from the environmental culture previously described, as that can be a larger group of Christians to interact with. This larger group of people provides the opportunity to give and receive care, interact and minister with a variety of people. The coaching component is a smaller, more personal group of people that can provide accountability and feedback to you.

Jesus demonstrated the value of coaching by personally training the twelve Apostles in addition to spending more intentional time with Peter, James and John.

> When morning came, he called his disciples to him and chose twelve of them, whom he also designated apostles... — **Luke 6:13**

> After six days Jesus took Peter, James and John with him and led them up a high mountain, where they were all alone. There he was transfigured before them. — **Mark 9:2**

NOTE: This *Discover Discipleship Course*, combined with the guidance of spiritually mature partners, is designed to help coach you spiritually.

It is helpful to receive all three types of discipleship training through the same church. This will ensure that what you are learning is consistent, thus limiting confusion in your spiritual development. It will also help you become fully engaged in a spiritual family rather than just partially engaged with several Christians.

An example of how to live this out practically would include:

- Attending weekly worship services to receive the teaching of God's word from gifted church leaders and teachers (instructional environment).

- Connecting to a sub-ministry or missional community in your church, to serve alongside and build closer relationships with other believers, outside of the church service environment (cultural learning).

- Developing strong accountability relationships with a mentor and a few other believers (coaching environment).

Note for Church Leaders: For additional information on how to establish systems for all three environments in your church, go to the *Church Leader Resources* page of **www.discoverdiscipleship.com**

1. Go back and identify the value of having each of these discipling environments in your life.

    - *Cultural*

    - *Instructional*

    - *Coaching*

2. How are these three discipling environments currently reflected in your life?

    - *Cultural*

    - *Instructional*

    - *Coaching*

why you need a spiritual family

As we learned in the previous lesson, in God's family we get spiritual support and oversight as we grow as His child. Even as a baby needs the loving care of a family, so every child of God needs the support and care of God's family.

You need the oversight of gifted, God-appointed elders and leaders. Christ has established His leadership in the church through the Apostles, Prophets, Evangelists, Pastors and Teachers, sometimes referred to as the *Five-Fold Ministry.* The *Five-Fold Ministry* leads by giving the church direction, solid doctrine, care and oversight. In the New Testament example, churches were led, shepherded—cared for—and taught by *groups* of these leaders, not just a single leader. These leadership groups were referred to as the elders of the church.[32]

The solid leadership that is given through Godly, gifted church elders and leaders is imperative for your spiritual growth. These leaders should prove themselves to be trustworthy by going through a system of examination and approval by other qualified leaders. This should include formal or informal training, as well as careful examination of the individual's gifts and character. Having a process to qualify elders helps to ensure that church leaders are both gifted and spiritually mature.[33]

Church leaders and elders should keep themselves accountable to each other as well as to other mature believers. No one in the body of Christ should be disconnected from others or "above" receiving direction from others.

Christians need the direction, care and solid doctrine that is given through qualified, Godly elders and leaders of a church. This is why meeting with a couple of friends, independent of a healthy church family and its leaders, isn't enough to provide appropriate spiritual oversight.

So Christ himself gave the apostles, the
prophets, the evangelists, the pastors and
teachers, to equip his people for works of
service, so that the body of Christ may be built
up until we all reach unity in the faith and in
the knowledge of the Son of God and become
mature, attaining to the whole measure of the
fullness of Christ. — **Ephesians 4:11-13**

1. **According to this verse, who placed the Five-Fold
   Ministry in the Church?**

2. **What is the purpose of the Five-Fold Ministry?**

You need mentors—spiritual mothers and fathers. It is
common for people today to disconnect from a spiritual family
and pick and select teaching and preaching from TV, the inter-
net, or other forms of media. Christian leadership described in
Scripture was relational. It was more than just instructional. It
was "life on life" learning. This is the value of spiritual mentors
in your life. [34]

A spiritual mentor might be a Sunday School teacher, a small group
leader or just a more mature, Godly friend. A spiritual mentor
does not have be a preacher or church leader, but they should be
shepherded by your church's Pastor or elders and leaders. Again,
receiving leadership from a mentor who is disconnected from a
church's leadership and oversight can be spiritually destructive.

Godly, spiritual mentors are people who know you and are known by you. They invest relationally in your life. Paul referred to himself as not just a teacher, but as a father.

> For if you were to have countless tutors in
> Christ, yet you would not have many fathers,
> for in Christ Jesus I became your father through
> the gospel. — 1 Corinthians 4:15 NASB

Scripture teaches the value of this by instructing the older men and women in the church to teach the younger (Titus 2:1-5). The context that is given is not so much "classroom teaching" as it is modeling and life teaching. (Reference the cultural and coaching environments we learned on *Day 24: Spiritual Growth Environments*.)

It should also be noted that you will never grow beyond the point of needing mentors in your life. The intensity of their role in your life might change as you mature, but we never "outgrow" the need for guidance and direction.[35]

3. What does it mean to invest relationally with others?

4. What do you think constitutes a spiritual mentor?

5. Do you have a spiritual mentor? If yes, list them. If no, what is keeping you from finding one?

You need the support of spiritual brothers and sisters.
Scripture insists that people need you and that you need people.
Following Jesus can be challenging. However, when you are connected to other believers you receive the support, encouragement
and accountability you need to make necessary changes. When
you try to go it alone your chance of failure is increased.

> Two are better than one, because they have a
> good return for their labor: if either of them
> falls down, one can help the other up. But pity
> anyone who falls and has no one to help them
> up. Also, if two lie down together, they will
> keep warm. But how can one keep warm alone?
> Though one may be overpowered, two can
> defend themselves. A cord of three strands is
> not quickly broken. — **Ecclesiastes 4:9-12**

In the family of God, we get the chance to learn what we may not
have learned in a natural family. We get to learn those things in a
community filled with grace and support.

Among other things, in God's family we learn how:

- to care for each other (Galatians 6:2).

- to handle conflict appropriately (Matthew 18:15-17).

- to support and encourage each other (1 Thessalonians 5:13).

- to restore each other if we fail (Galatians 6:1).

- to love each other despite our shortcomings (Ephesians 4:32,
  Colossians 3:13).

- to pray for each other (James 5:16).

- to view and serve each other as Christ viewed and served
  the world (Philippians 2:1-11).

- to give and receive forgiveness (Colossians 3:13).

- to share the responsibility of the church and Jesus' mission
  on earth (1 Corinthians 12:27).

NOTE: Grace and support does not mean that people in the church should condone sinful behavior in your life. It does mean that you are given a chance to learn and grow as long as you demonstrate willingness to learn and grow. Even if you quit, you are still loved. When you demonstrate willingness to return to Jesus' ways, you are accepted back with grace and given a new opportunity.

6. List some reasons you should develop relationships with Christian brothers and sisters.

the church needs you

In the New Testament, there are over 50 direct commands for the church to do something for one another.[36] We cannot do the "one-another commands" of Scripture if we are not around one another.

1. **Reread the bulleted list from yesterday that describes values learned and provided in a healthy church family. Which ones stand out to you? Why?**

We have a shared responsibility in creating a healthy church family. Most people want to be loved, forgiven, encouraged and cared for. But the question is, are you willing to do this for another person? In other words, *are you looking for the benefit of a spiritual family without sharing the responsibility of a spiritual family?*

Scripture teaches that the family of God is like a body. Each part is dependent on the other parts. This means that not only do you need people, but they need what you have to offer as well. God leaves deficits in our lives that can only be filled through the strengths of others. He designed us this way so we will not forget our need for others. (Refer to the interdependent relationships we learned about on *Day 4: The Confined Attitude.*)

> As it is, there are many parts, but one body. The eye cannot say to the hand, "I don't need you!" And the head cannot say to the feet, "I don't need you!" — **1 Corinthians 12:20-21**

2. What is your reaction to the truth that people need you?

Not only do you need leadership, mentorship and support in your life, people need these things from you as well. As we read in the previous day's lesson in Ephesians 4:11-13, God expects *you* to mature and grow. As you mature and grow, your responsibilities increase.

God expects you to mature and care for others. Notice in the following passage, the writer of Hebrews reprimands those who should be teaching others, but instead desire to be fed milk. In other words, they refuse to grow up and assume responsibility.

> You have been believers so long now that you ought to be teaching others. Instead, you need someone to teach you again the basic things about God's word. You are like babies who need milk and cannot eat solid food.
> — Hebrews 5:12 NLT

This is God's vision for His family: mature "mothers and fathers" mentoring "sons and daughters" into "mothers and fathers" who care for new "sons and daughters".

3. What questions and concerns do you have with the idea that God expects you to mature and care for others?

You do not have to be an "upfront" Bible teacher in order to help others grow spiritually. As you mature and invest in others, the example of your life will bring the biggest impact and lessons to others. Tomorrow's lesson will explore spiritual maturity in more detail.

God has given you gifts to build up the church.

> A spiritual gift is given to each of us so we can help each other. — **1 Corinthians 12:7 NLT**

We will explore this in detail in *Workbook 6: Discover Alignment.* For now, it suffices to say, that God has given you abilities that will benefit His Church. He has designed the body of Christ to need each other (1 Corinthians 12:20-21).

maturity and mentoring

STAGES OF SPIRITUAL MATURITY

Spiritual maturity has more to do with becoming like Jesus than with physical age. Someone may be physically younger than you but more spiritually mature. Within our spiritual families we can find people who are spiritual parents, spiritual teens and spiritual children.[37]

> I write to you, dear children, because you know the Father.
>
> I write to you, fathers, because you know him who is from the beginning.
>
> I write to you, young men, because you are strong, and the word of God lives in you, and you have overcome the evil one.
> — 1 John 2:14

Spiritual Parents. People with a maturing relationship with Jesus, who have led someone else to faith and are helping them grow into a disciple or have "adopted" a young Christian to help them grow into a disciple of Jesus. As previously stated, it is God's desire for all of us to mature into spiritual mothers and fathers who can care and mentor new Christians.

Spiritual Teens. People who are growing in their faith in Jesus by learning and applying basic spiritual principles; are overcoming spiritual strongholds in their lives; are assuming some responsibility in their spiritual family; and who can also assist in discipling younger Christians. They may have led people to faith in the Lord but lack the spiritual maturity, or gifts and abilities, to begin discipling others on their own.

Spiritual Children. New Christians who have received new life in Christ and are learning to grow in their faith in Jesus. Spiritual children are spiritually immature and "weaker" in the faith. We should be patient with them as they grow up in their new life in God. This doesn't mean we should not speak truth to them. It means we should demonstrate patience and give support as they are maturing and learning to apply truth.

> And we urge you, brothers and sisters, warn
> those who are idle and disruptive, encourage
> the disheartened, help the weak, be patient with
> everyone. — 1 Thessalonians 5:14

1. At which of the three stages of spiritual maturity do you think you are? Explain:

MENTORING CAUTIONS

People often fall into two extremes when it comes to mentoring others.

Carelessness. Some approach mentoring and leading carelessly. They assume just because someone is gifted, it gives them a right to influence and lead others in the body of Christ. This is not necessarily true. With giftedness, must also come maturity.

Think about it like this, just because a person has the biological ability to father or mother a child, does not mean they have the maturity to care for a child. Maturity takes time and experience to develop.

In order to lead in the church a person must also grow in their character and Christlikeness, not just in their gifts and callings from God. This is why Paul warned not to put a new believer into church leadership.

> He must not be a recent convert, or he may become conceited and fall under the same judgment as the devil. — 1 Timothy 3:6

Let's also note, simply because someone has been in the church for a long time, does not mean they are growing spiritually. Due to weakness in Bible Study and prayer, and failure to overcome strongholds in their life, they could still be classified as a spiritual "child". They should grow and spiritually mature before they lead.

As we learned in *Workbook 2: Discover Freedom*, the process of overcoming the devil in our lives causes us to mature. We must grow strong in the Word and strong in overcoming the evil one. This enables us to lead others. This does not mean a new believer cannot bring others to the Lord, it simply means they are not prepared to lead them in growing in their spiritual growth. This will take some help from other mature believers.

Fear. The second mentoring mistake that people make, is being afraid to mentor others. They are afraid of making a mistake, teaching something wrong, or failing other people. While some have too much confidence, others lack enough confidence.

As we have already stated, growing in the Word of God and in overcoming the devil will enable you to mature and help others. Remember you do not have to be a Bible teacher to mentor others, but you must present the example of a life submitted to the Lord.

Here are a few factors that will allow you to become a good mentor to others:

- Overcome personal spiritual strongholds.

- Develop the habit of learning and applying Scripture.

- Learn to discern the voice of God.

- Have good, Godly support to help you mentor others.

- Go through training and be teachable.

- Have a good teaching curriculum that can help guide your conversations as you mentor others.

The last factor —a good curriculum—can assist people who are not strong Bible teachers, to be able to help others learn and grow. This was one of the main goals for creating the *Discover Discipleship Course.* Using these materials, along with having a more mature Christian to consult if you have questions, will help you mentor others.

Again, the point is, the formal teaching aspects of discipleship can come in a variety of ways. One of the most important things you can provide to others is the example of a good Godly life.

2. Review the bulleted list above. Rate yourself in each of these areas and explain. Specifically, how can you grow in the weak areas?

3. What are your thoughts, fears or concerns about leading others?

fostering a healthy church environment

Since the church is the family of God, Scripture teaches us that we should view and treat the other people in the church as family members.

> Never speak harshly to an older man, but appeal to him respectfully as you would to your own father. Talk to younger men as you would to your own brothers. Treat older women as you would your mother, and treat younger women with all purity as you would your own sisters. — I Timothy 5:1-2 NLT

1. How would the church be different if people followed this Scriptural instruction?

2. How would you treat others differently if you followed this command?

A COMMUNITY OF RESPECT AND SUBMISSION

As indicated in the previous passage of Scripture, the family of God is a community of submission and respect.

We are to live lives of mutual submission and respect to each other out of respect for Christ.

> Submit to one another out of reverence for Christ. — **Ephesians 5:21**

Read Philippians 2:1-11.

3. **Based on Philippians 2:1-11, describe what our attitude toward other believers should be:**

We are to have confidence in spiritual leaders and submit to their leadership and vision.

> Have confidence in your leaders and submit to their authority, because they keep watch over you as those who must give an account. Do this so that their work will be a joy, not a burden, for that would be of no benefit to you.
> — **Hebrews 13:17**

The word submission can be understood to mean *come under* a mission. Becoming part of a church family means that you support, or *come under,* the mission and vision of your church and its God-appointed leaders. In a group, everyone does not always get their way. A group must be unified around a vision. If you begin to have competing visions, it creates division. The suffix "di" *means more than one.*[38] Division literally means *many visions.*

Respect and submission mean honor. The biblical word for honor in the following passage means *to place value.* [39] We are to value and care for spiritual leaders who direct the affairs of the church well, humbly submitting to their oversight.

> The elders who direct the affairs of the church
> well are worthy of double honor, especially
> those whose work is preaching and teaching.
> — 1 Timothy 5:17

Respect and submission mean submitting yourself to the spiritual correction of others. Your church leaders and family have a Scriptural obligation to challenge you on sin and help bring you back onto the right path.

> Brothers and sisters, if someone is caught in a
> sin, you who live by the Spirit should restore
> that person gently. But watch yourselves, or
> you also may be tempted. Carry each other's
> burdens, and in this way you will fulfill the law
> of Christ. — **Galatians 6:1-2**

Respect and submission does not mean blindly doing whatever someone tells you to do. Obviously, if a church leader is abusive or attempts to cause you to sin, you should not follow their leadership; however, you should find Godly leadership to follow.

Respect and submission means directing concerns to appropriate people. As we have previously learned on *Day 19: Biblical Conflict Resolution,* you should talk to the person with whom you have a conflict. This also means that if you have a conflict or concern with your church's mission or leadership, you should address this with the appropriate leaders of your church and seek resolution with them to avoid spreading division in the church body.

Divisiveness is not the same as disagreement. Divisiveness under-mines the vision of a church through handling disagreements in an unscriptural manner. Being divisive in a church is Scriptural grounds to be asked to leave that church.

> Warn a divisive person once, and then warn
> them a second time. After that, have nothing to
> do with them. — **Titus 3:10**

4. Review the concepts about Respect and Submission. What stands out to you and why?

factors that block christian community

RELATIONAL ATTITUDES

In the second section of this book, we learned several different relational attitudes that block companionship in relationships. These attitudes will limit or prohibit your ability to connect with a church family.

The Confined Attitude can keep you isolated and keep you unaware of your need for Christian relationships. Church might be viewed as unnecessary or will just be a place you go to rather than a family you are part of.

The Codependent Attitude can cause you to look to the church or someone in the church as your "savior" that will solve all of your problems. It is also easy to become a "savior" to people who need help.

The Controlling Attitude can cause you to try to force other people to do the right thing. You might start assuming too much responsibility for the spiritual growth of others and try to force change, rather than lovingly confronting people with the truth, and supporting their change.

The Critical Attitude can cause you to find fault with every-one and every church. Relationships in a church family will be short-lived or miserable, because people are not _____ enough for you.

The Crisis Attitude can cause you to be easily offended. You might go into a church family thinking they are the "perfect" church family, but then quickly become angry when someone cannot meet your expectations.

The Competitive Attitude can cause you to see your church or ministry as better than others. Trying to outpace others or get recognition for accomplishments can motivate your actions, rather than love for God and others. This can cause you to ignore relationships and seek accomplishments. It can also produce jealousy of others in the church or jealousy of other ministries or church congregations.

The Consumeristic Attitude can cause you to see the church as existing to meet your needs. Rather than a family where love and responsibility is shared, you can begin to demand that the church meet your needs while you refuse to help others.

The Comfortable Attitude can cause you to only connect with people who are like you, or only when you feel like it. Scripture gives us a command to be one with people who are different from us.

1. Identify the Relational Attitudes you personally struggle with. *(Refer to Appendix 2)*. Note how each can keep you from connecting to a church family.

A REBELLIOUS HEART

In the previous lesson we learned that the Church is a community of mutual respect and submission. Many of these unchecked relational attitudes will lead to a rebellious heart that will prohibit us from connecting to a spiritual family or cause us to be divisive within our church family. Fault finding, needing to be in control, and always believing we are right are a few things that can lead to a rebellious heart and keep us separated from a church family.

God's people in the Old Testament, the nation of Israel, were constantly rebelling against the direction of their spiritual leaders. This brought God's anger. In the book of Hebrews, we are reminded to not harden our hearts as these people did. We are challenged to submit to the oversight of God's church.

Don't harden your hearts as Israel did when
they rebelled, when they tested me in the
wilderness. — **Hebrews 3:8 NLT**

Have confidence in your leaders and submit to
their authority, because they keep watch over
you as those who must give an account. Do this
so that their work will be a joy, not a burden, for
that would be of no benefit to you.
— **Hebrews 13:17**

As stated before, we should not blindly trust everyone, however, we should find church leaders and a church family we trust and follow their lead.

2. **What does it mean to be spiritually rebellious?**

3. **Can we truly say that we are surrendered to Jesus but live in rebellion against Godly leadership? Explain:**

BUSYNESS

The truth is, nearly everyone lives busy hectic lives these days. It can be easy to neglect your spiritual life and allow the "cares of this life" to choke out God's purposes in your life. As noted before, Christian community is not just for people who have the time or need some friends. It is God's desire for all of us to be an active part of His family.

We must make an intentional effort to connect with others. This means time for corporate worship services as well taking time to mentor and be mentored. You are in control of your schedule. You have to decide in advance what is most important and make the family of God a priority. This will mean rearranging some things as well as eliminating other things from your schedule.

We must take time to engage with what will bring and foster spiritual growth. We can no longer be driven by what the "world" says is important. Living in our created design as God's child must become our priority. This created design includes taking time for the family of God.

> Still others, like seed sown among thorns,
> hear the word; but the worries of this life, the
> deceitfulness of wealth and the desires for other
> things come in and choke the word, making it
> unfruitful. — **Mark 4:18-19**

4. **In what ways does busyness keep you from connecting to the body of Christ?**

5. **What is your plan to address this?**

FEAR/DISTRUST

Fear of being hurt, or being hurt again, keeps many people distant from others. Relational pain is difficult and relational hurt that comes through church seems to be even more difficult to handle. As you take time to connect with a spiritual family, remember what you have learned in this book. It is unwise to trust everyone but learn to give people opportunity to earn your trust. Also, be patient with others. Go back and review the principles of conflict resolution and the relational agreement we engaged with on *Day 22: Tips for Healthy Conflict Resolution.* These principles will help you as you develop new relationships in a church.

Also, remember to pray and ask the Holy Spirit to guide you as you begin forming new relationships.

> Make allowance for each other's faults, and forgive anyone who offends you. Remember, the Lord forgave you, so you must forgive others. — **Colossians 3:13 NLT**

6. **What is keeping you from trusting people in your church family?**

7. **What is your next step in overcoming this?**

the power of christian unity

Christian unity can be difficult, but when followers of Jesus learn to be unified, Jesus is present, and God's Power is displayed. Unity within the church is to be valued above everything. Notice what the following passages teach us about unity:

> Therefore, as God's chosen people, holy and dearly loved, clothe yourselves with compassion, kindness, humility, gentleness and patience. Bear with each other and forgive one another if any of you has a grievance against someone. Forgive as the Lord forgave you. *And over all these virtues put on love, which binds them all together in perfect unity.* — **Colossians 3:12-14** *(Emphasis added)*

> Be completely humble and gentle; be patient, bearing with one another in love. *Make every effort to keep the unity of the Spirit through the bond of peace.* — **Ephesians 4:2-3** *(Emphasis added)*

1. **What stands out to you in the preceding two passages?**

Unity does not always mean agreeing with each other; it is not achieved by pretending that everything is agreeable when it is not. Unity does not mean that everyone gets their way. Unity can actually involve learning to work together *despite differences.*

2. What stands out to you in the preceding paragraph?

While it might be difficult to achieve at times, the pay-off for Christian unity is powerful.

> My prayer is not for them alone. I pray also for those who will believe in me through their message, that all of them may be one, Father, just as you are in me and I am in you. May they also be in us *so that the world may believe that you have sent me.* — **John 17:20-21** *(Emphasis added)*

3. According to the preceding passage, what is the result of being one with other believers in God?

Again, truly I tell you that if two of you on earth agree about anything they ask for, it will be done for them by my Father in heaven. For where two or three gather in my name, there am I with them. — **Matthew 18:19-20**

4. **According to the preceding passage, what did Jesus say would happen when believers agree together in His Name?**

Unity within your local congregation. Working for unity in the local congregation you are part of is essential to your church fulfilling its God-given mission in your community. We have already discussed in detail the importance of submission to one another and to church leaders, as well as the need to not allow disagreements to turn into division.

Remember, it is not a question of what you will do *if* you have a disagreement, but rather what you will do *when* you have a disagreement. Use the principles of conflict resolution you have learned in this workbook.

God does lead people out of one congregation into another congregation, but do not allow disagreements to drive you out. Do your best to resolve any disagreement before you leave a congregation. Remember Jesus taught us to settle our disputes with our brothers before we bring our gifts to the Lord.

> Therefore if you are presenting your offering at the altar, and there remember that your brother has something against you, leave your offering there before the altar and go; first be reconciled to your brother, and then come and present your offering. — Matthew 5:23-24

Notice in this passage, Jesus taught that even if your brother is not doing the right thing in seeking reconciliation, you should take the first step.

5. Are there currently any unresolved issues between you and other Christians, pastors or churches? If yes, what is your next step in seeking resolution to the conflict? (Review Matthew 18:15-17.)

Unity with other church congregations. Our view of church is often confined to the local congregation or denomination that we are part of. While it is important to be part of a local congregation, remember God's view is bigger.

Many of the New Testament letters were not written to just one congregation, but to a multitude of home congregations scattered around a region. So, in essence, God was addressing the Church of the region.

It is important for us to have a grasp of what God desires to do in our city or region, how other congregations are part of this, and how we can work together for the greater Kingdom good.

This is not to say that we should unite with everyone who claims the name of Christ. Jesus said many would call Him Lord, but He does not know them (Matthew 7:21-23). This is a simple acknowledgment that many times as Christians there are matters that should not divide us as deeply as they do.

As Christians, we do not have to agree on everything in order to pray or serve the world together. We can even think our brother or sister is wrong about some issues, but if we agree about the Lordship of Jesus and are willing to express some grace and Christian love for each other, then we could do a lot of good for the Kingdom of God together.

6. **What are ways that your church can connect with other churches in your city or regions?**

what's next?

Congratulations on making it to the end of this Workbook! You have gained some valuable tools, skills, and practices to help you approach earthly relationships the way God intended.

In the next Workbook, *Workbook 5: Discover Mission*, you will learn how to engage in Jesus' Mission to reconcile the world to God. You will learn practical ways to reach out and share the love of God to the world. This will help alleviate fears and misconceptions about what it means to bring new people into God's family.

You are on an exciting journey of discovering and growing in your identity as a Child of God. Keep pushing forward.

> Brothers and sisters, I do not consider myself yet to have taken hold of it. But one thing I do: Forgetting what is behind and straining toward what is ahead, I press on toward the goal to win the prize for which God has called me heavenward in Christ Jesus.
> — **Philippians 3:13-14**

WORKBOOK 4:

relationships checkpoint

1. Have you identified the primary *Relational Attitudes* you tend to approach others with? List them here:

2. Have you made a complete *Amends List* of people you have hurt and people who have hurt you? If no, what is keeping you from this?

3. Have you already gone to at least one person on your *Amends List* and asked for or given forgiveness (depending on which was necessary)? If no, what is keeping you from this?

4. Is there an unresolved conflict in your life right now? If so, what step of Matthew 18:15-17 are you currently on?

5. If you are coming to our church from another church, have you had a conversation with your former pastor about your decision to leave?

6. Are you leaving due to unresolved conflict with that church? If so, what is your next step to resolve it? (Based on Matthew 18:15-17)

7. Who is your church's small group leader?

8. Go back and review your *Plan for Change* from *Book 2: Discover Freedom.* When will you review this plan again with your accountability partner?

notes

appendices

APPENDIX 1
substitute identities & scriptures

I am defined by what I can do or achieve.

Even youths grow tired and weary, and young men stumble and fall; but those who hope in the LORD will renew their strength. They will soar on wings like eagles; they will run and not grow weary, they will walk and not be faint.
— Isaiah 40:30

I once thought these things were valuable, but now I consider them worthless because of what Christ has done. Yes, everything else is worthless when compared with the infinite value of knowing Christ Jesus my Lord. For his sake I have discarded everything else, counting it all as garbage, so that I could gain Christ.
— Philippians 3:7-8 NLT

Whatever you do, do your work heartily, as for the Lord rather than for men.
— Colossians 3:23 NASB

ABILITIES

I am defined by a skill or ability that I have.

> You may say to yourself, "My power and the strength of my hands have produced this wealth for me." But remember the LORD your God, for it is he who gives you the ability to produce wealth, and so confirms his covenant, which he swore to your ancestors, as it is today.
> **—Deuteronomy 8:17-18**

> For by the grace given me I say to every one of you: Do not think of yourself more highly than you ought, but rather think of yourself with sober judgment, in accordance with the faith God has distributed to each of you.
> **— Romans 12:3**

> Therefore, as the Scriptures say, "If you want to boast, boast only about the LORD."
> **— 1 Corinthians 1:31 NLT**

POSSESSIONS

I am defined by what I own.

> Then he said to them, "Watch out! Be on your guard against all kinds of greed; a man's life does not consist in the abundance of his possessions." **— Luke 12:15**

> Keep your lives free from the love of money and be content with what you have, because God has said, "Never will I leave you; never will I forsake you." **— Hebrews 13:5**

> No one can serve two masters. Either he will hate the one and love the other, or he will be devoted to the one and despise the other. You cannot serve both God and Money.
> **— Matthew 6:24**

Therefore I tell you, do not worry about your life, what you will eat or drink; or about your body, what you will wear. Is not life more important than food, and the body more important than clothes? —**Matthew 6:25**

APPEARANCE

I am defined by how I look.

Charm is deceptive, and beauty is fleeting; but a woman who fears the LORD is to be praised. — **Proverbs 31:30**

For women who claim to be devoted to God should make themselves attractive by the good things they do. — **1 Timothy 2:10 NLT**

APPROVAL

I am defined by who accepts me.

I'm not interested in crowd approval. And do you know why? Because I know you and your crowds. I know that love, especially God's love, is not on your working agenda. — **John 5:41-42 MSG**

Peter and the other apostles replied: "We must obey God rather than men! — **Acts 5:29**

Am I now trying to win the approval of human beings, or of God? Or am I trying to please people? If I were still trying to please people, I would not be a servant of Christ. — **Galatians 1:10**

On the contrary, we speak as men approved by God to be entrusted with the gospel. We are not trying to please men but God, who tests our hearts. — **1 Thessalonians 2:4**

We were not looking for praise from people, not from you or anyone else, even though as apostles of Christ we could have asserted our authority. — **1 Thessalonians 2:6**

Blessed are you when people insult you, persecute you and falsely say all kinds of evil against you because of me. Rejoice and be glad, because great is your reward in heaven, for in the same way they persecuted the prophets who were before you. — **Matthew 5:11-12**

AFFECTION

I am defined by who loves me.

...all things (including you) have been created through him (Jesus) and for him (Jesus).
— **Colossians 1:16b**

The Lord appeared to us in the past, saying: "I have loved you with an everlasting love; I have drawn you with unfailing kindness.
— **Jeremiah 31:3**

For I am convinced that neither death nor life, neither angels nor demons, neither the present nor the future, nor any powers, neither height nor depth, nor anything else in all creation, will be able to separate us from the love of God that is in Christ Jesus our Lord. —**Romans 8:38-39**

ATTENTION

I am defined by being noticed for positive or negative behavior, or by getting sympathy from others.

How can you believe since you accept glory from one another but do not seek the glory that comes from the only God? — **John 5:44**

Do nothing out of selfish ambition or vain conceit. Rather, in humility value others above yourselves. — **Philippians 2:3**

Be careful not to practice your righteousness in front of others to be seen by them. If you do, you will have no reward from your Father in heaven. — **Matthew 6:1**

POWER

I am defined by being in control.

Son of man, say to the ruler of Tyre, "This is what the Sovereign LORD says: In the pride of your heart you say, "I am a god; I sit on the throne of a god in the heart of the seas.' But you are a man and not a god, though you think you are as wise as a god." — **Ezekiel 28:2**

Trust in the LORD with all your heart and lean not on your own understanding; in all your ways submit to him, and he will make your paths straight. — **Proverbs 3:5-6**

Look to the LORD and his strength; seek his face always. — **1 Chronicles 16:11**

… "Not by might nor by power but by my Spirit" says the Lord God Almighty.
— **Zechariah 4:6b**

There is no one holy like the LORD; there is no one besides you; there is no Rock like our God.
— **1 Samuel 2:2**

APPETITES

I am defined by my desires. These can be natural desires such as those for food or sex or acquired desires such as those for drugs and alcohol.

Appetite for food

"My food," said Jesus, "is to do the will of him who sent me and to finish his work."
— **John 4:34**

I know what it is to be in need, and I know what it is to have plenty. I have learned the secret of being content in any and every situation, whether well fed or hungry, whether living in plenty or in want. I can do everything through him who gives me strength.
— **Philippians 4:12-13**

Their destiny is destruction, their god is their stomach, and their glory is in their shame. Their mind is on earthly things. — **Philippians 3:19**

Sexual appetite

".... How then could I do such a wicked thing and sin against God?" (Joseph's response to sexual temptation.) — **Genesis 39:9b**

Flee from sexual immorality. All other sins a person commits are outside the body, but whoever sins sexually, sins against their own body. Do you not know that your bodies are temples of the Holy Spirit, who is in you, whom you have received from God? You are not your own; you were bought at a price. Therefore honor God with your bodies.
— **1 Corinthians 6:18-20**

Appetite for alcohol or other drugs.

Do not get drunk on wine, which leads to debauchery. Instead, be filled with the Spirit.
— **Ephesians 5:18**

Wine is a mocker and beer a brawler; whoever is led astray by them is not wise.
— **Proverbs 20:1**

PLEASURE

I am defined by being comfortable and feeling good.

But he will pour out his anger and wrath on those who live for themselves, who refuse to obey the truth and instead live lives of wickedness. — **Romans 2:8 NLT**

And I'll say to myself, "You have plenty of grain laid up for many years. Take life easy; eat, drink and be merry." But God said to him, "You fool! This very night your life will be demanded from you. Then who will get what you have prepared for yourself?"
— **Luke 12:19-20**

APPENDIX 2
relational attitude assessment

CONFINED ATTITUDE

1. Do you prefer being by yourself to being with others?

2. Do you believe that your survival and success in life has been mostly by your own effort?

3. Do you feel weak or lazy when you ask for help?

CODEPENDENT ATTITUDE

1. Do you fear being alone, even if the relationship is harmful?

2. Do you find that you expect others to do things for you that you can do yourself? Or do you find yourself consistently doing for others what they can do for themselves?

3. Do you get very anxious or upset if you think someone is unhappy with you?

CONTROLLING ATTITUDE

1. Do you often find yourself trying to "force" someone do what you think is right (excluding your small children)?

2. Do you feel responsible to make sure people around you have good outcomes in their life choices? Or do you often feel personally responsible when someone in your life makes a poor choice?

3. Do you feel the need to "clean up" after others make bad choices?

CRITICAL ATTITUDE

1. Do you tend to mentally or verbally criticize others around you?

2. Do you tend to have a strong opinion about things, even if you do not "voice" them?

3. When giving advice, is your motivation fueled by being proud of what you know?

CRISIS ATTITUDE

1. Do you often have a new story to tell of someone who has done you wrong?

2. Do you find that a lot of your relationships end negatively over a disagreement?

3. Do you believe that you are stuck in your position in life and cannot change your situation?

COMPETITIVE ATTITUDE

1. Does it make you happy when you perform better than someone else at any given task?

2. Are you jealous of others' lifestyle, possessions, and/or relationships?

3. Do you think often about how your performance compares to someone else's performance at any task?

CONSUMERISTIC ATTITUDE

1. Do you view the relationships in your life as a means to get what you want?

2. Do you typically expect something in return if you do something good for someone?

3. Are you often accused of treating others poorly, or accused of "looking down" upon others?

COMFORTABLE ATTITUDE

1. Are most of your relationships with people who are similar to you in age, personality, life choices, race, etc.?

2. Do you avoid people who are different from you in age, personality, life choices, race, etc.?

3. Do you have strong, negative opinions about groups of people who are different from you, even if you have limited experience interacting with them?

INSTRUCTIONS

☐ Go back and circle the name of each Relational Attitude category that you answered yes to more than two questions in.

☐ If you answered yes to more than two questions in a Relational Attitude category, you probably struggle with this attitude. List all that you struggle with:

APPENDIX 3

a relational agreement

1. I will contribute to this relationship, not only receive from it.

2. When in doubt, I will give you the "benefit of the doubt." I will not automatically assume that you meant to hurt me.

3. If I ever wonder about your actions, I will not talk ABOUT you; I will talk TO you about it, quickly.

4. I will not allow others to talk about you behind your back. I will only discuss our problems with others if am seeking help with mediation or intervention.

5. When I speak with you, I will try to keep my emotions in check and I will refrain from name-calling, accusing and belittling.

6. When you are speaking to me, I will allow you to do so honestly but not brutally. I will do my best to focus on what you are saying and verify that I understand you accurately.

7. I will value our relationship more than our disagreements.

8. If we cannot find a resolution, we will bring our conflict to _____ and allow them to mediate it for us.

9. I will always work toward forgiving you. However, your actions may destroy my trust in you.

10. If I break any of these commitments, please remind me of this agreement and I will do the same for you.

Signed: _____

notes

ENDNOTES

[1] Bilezikian, Gilbert. *Community 101: Reclaiming the Church as Community of Oneness.* Grand Rapids, MI.: Zondervan Publishing House, 1993. Pg. 27

[2] Ibid. Pg. 32-34

[3] https://www.dictionary.com/browse/com

[4] Oxford Dictionaries Online: https://en.oxforddictionaries.com/definition/confined

[5] Oxford Dictionaries Online: https://en.oxforddictionaries.com/definition/co-dependent

[6] Baker, John. *Celebrate Recovery Leader's Guide.* Grand Rapids, MI.: Zondervan. 1998. Pg. 232

[7] Oxford Dictionaries Online: https://en.oxforddictionaries.com/definition/control

[8] Cloud, Henry and John Townsend. "The Law of Reaping and Sowing." FaithGateway. https://www.faithgateway.com/the-law-of-reaping-and-sowing/#.XJ_x0y-ZOMA

[9] Oxford Dictionaries Online: https://en.oxforddictionaries.com/definition/critical

[10] https://www.blueletterbible.org/lang/lexicon/lexicon.cfm?Strongs=G2919&t=KJV

[11] Oxford Dictionaries Online: https://en.oxforddictionaries.com/definition/crisis

[12] Epp, John Van. *How to Avoid Falling in Love with a Jerk: The Foolproof Way to Follow Your Heart without Losing Your Mind.* New York: McGraw-Hill, 2008. Pg. 21-24

[13] Baker, John and Richard D. Warren. *Life's Healing Choices: Freedom from Your Hurts, Hang-ups, and Habits.* New York, NY: Howard Books., 2007. Pg. 7

[14] Oxford Dictionaries Online: https://en.oxforddictionaries.com/definition/competitive

[15] Oxford Dictionaries Online: https://en.oxforddictionaries.com/definition/consume

[16] Oxford Dictionaries Online: https://en.oxforddictionaries.com/definition/comfortable

[17] Neighbour, Ralph. *The Arrival Kit: A Guide for Your Journey in the Kingdom of God.* Houston, TX: TOUCH Publications. Pg. 90

[18] Luke 6:12-16: Luke 8:1-3: Luke 10:1

[19] Covey, Stephen R. *The 7 Habits of Highly Effective People.* London: Pocket Books, 2004. Habit 5: Seek First to Understand, Then to Be Understood.

[20] Hogue, Rodney. *Forgiveness.* Hayward, CA: Community of Grace. 2008. Pg. 13-18

[21] https://www.blueletterbible.org/lang/lexicon/lexicon.cfm?Strongs=G863&t=KJV

[22] Keller, Timothy. *The Reason for God: Belief in an Age of Skepticism.* Penguin, 2016. Pg. 185-188

[23] Much of the content of both Amends Lesson was inspired by: Baker, John and Richard D. Warren. *Life's Healing Choices: Freedom from Your Hurts, Hang-ups, and Habits.* New York, NY: Howard Books. 2007. Choice Four: Coming Clean. Also see: Baker, John. *Celebrate Recovery Leader's Guide.* Grand Rapids, MI.: Zondervan. 1998.

[24] Cloud, Henry, and John Townsend. *Boundaries: When to Say Yes, How to Say No to Take Control of Your Life.* Grand Rapids, MI: Zondervan, 2004.

[25] Claiborne, Shane, and Haw, Chris. (2008). *Jesus for President.* Grand Rapids, MI: Zondervan. Kindle locations 739-784. This "third way" teaching was influenced by the reseach of Wink, Walter. *Jesus and Nonviolence: A Third Way.* Minneapolis, MN: Augsburg Fortress, 2003. Pg. 12-26. While the author does not support all of Mr. Wink's teachings, Mr. Wink's cited research of the culture of Jesus provides a unique perspective on Jesus' teachings in Matthew 5:38-42.

[26] Walker, John. "Gary Smalley: 'LUV' talk is key to marital success." Baptist Press. http://bpnews.net/10325

[27] Ibid.

[28] Ibid.

[29] Luke 10:1; Luke 6:12-16; Matthew 17:1-8

[30] Breen, Mike. *Leading Missional Communities.* Kindle Edition: 3DM. 2013. Kindle Locations 1336-1359

[31] Ibid. Kindle Locations 102-160.

[32] Biblical examples of groups of elders leading the church: Acts 11:30; Acts 15:4; Acts 20:28; Acts 21:8; 1 Timothy 4:14; 1 Timothy 5:17,19; Titus 1:5-9; 1 Peter 5:1-4.

[33] Contemporary churches have varying responsibilities and qualifications for church elders. Since the elders' responsibility is to spiritually lead the church which goes beyond simply making "business' decisions, elders should be spiritually mature. For Biblical qualifications for elders read Titus 1:5-9.

[34] Chan, Francis and Beuving, Mark. *Multiply: Disciples Making Disciples*. Colorado Springs, CO: David C. Cook. 2012. Pg. 16-17

[35] Ibid, Pg. 33

[36] https://overviewbible.com/one-another-infographic/

[37] Neighbour, Pg. 14-19

[38] https://www.dictionary.com/browse/di-

[39] https://www.blueletterbible.org/lang/lexicon/lexicon.cfm?Strongs=G5092&t=ESV

Workbook 4: Relationships Checkpoint —Icon made by Roundicons from Flaticon is licensed by Creative Commons BY 3.0

notes

Discover Discipleship Course

1. IDENTITY

2. FREEDOM

3. GROWTH

4. RELATIONSHIPS

5. MISSION

6. ALIGNMENT

For purchasing information and bulk discounts
go to discoverdiscipleship.com

Made in the USA
Middletown, DE
07 November 2023

42108388R00091